GW00363841

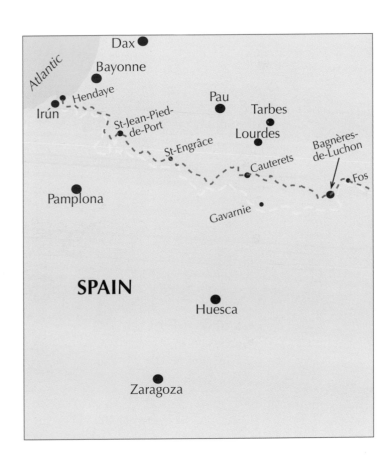

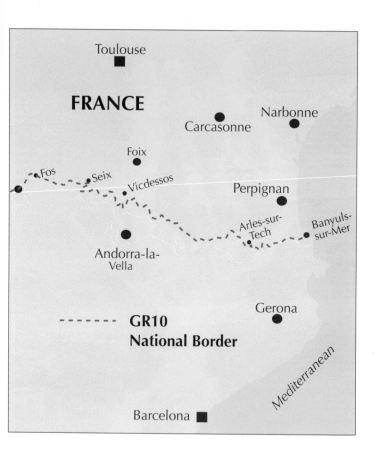

Toulouse

FRANCE

Carcasonne

Narbonne

Foix

Fos

Seix

Vicdessos

Perpignan

Arles-sur-
Tech

Banyuls-
sur-Mer

Andorra-la-
Vella

Gerona

- - - - - - **GR10**
National Border

Mediterranean

Barcelona

Cascade below Pic du Midi d'Ossau (Day 13)

Tm B				Cp 10		
hr	Coin Love	Makes	km	Coin Love	Makes	
$18\tfrac{1}{4}$	1318	1478	20.5	254	1001	
18	454	1316	2.15	342		
12	528	1001	30.3	135	737	
18	1250	400	12.1	1518	1350	
15	889	828	30	848	828	
30	1410	345	1.31	214	1788	
12	212	450	45	447	1840	

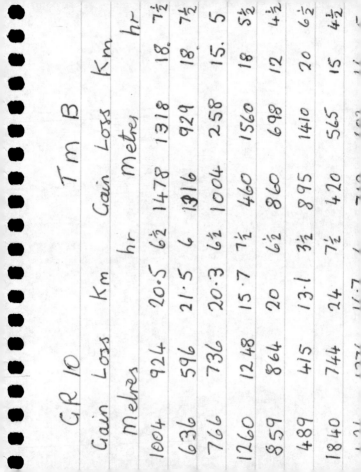

	GR 10				Tm B		
Gain Metres	Loss	Km	hr	Gain Metres	Loss	Km	hr
1004	924	20·5	6½	1478	1318	18.	7½
636	596	21·5	6	1316	929	18	7½
766	736	20·3	6½	1004	258	15.	5
1260	1248	15·7	7½	460	1560	18	5½
859	864	20	6½	860	698	12	4½
489	415	13·1	3½	895	1410	20	6½
1840	744	24	7½	420	565	15	4½

	4	6½
	8	17
	257	1546
	733	772
	4½	5
	12·3	15·1
	165	1090
1811	1185	340

THE GR10 TRAIL
COAST TO COAST THROUGH THE FRENCH PYRENEES

AUTHOR PROFILE

When asked to describe my father, the word indomitable invariably springs to mind. Dad's exploits provided a thread of marvellous adventure throughout our otherwise ordinary upbringing.

He first visited the Pyrenees more than 35 years ago and then, a few years later, returned on honeymoon. The majestic and diverse mountains caught his imagination but it was not until 1987 that he began to revisit them in earnest, first with the whole family, and later with interested friends. He undertook a number of solo trips when collecting material for the guide to the GR11, *Through the Spanish Pyrenees*, published in 1996 (revised 1999). For the revision, he walked the entire length of the trail in one expedition with his son.

When not in the mountains, dad, who lives in retirement in Shropshire, spends his time constructing a new model railway (complete with Pyrenean castle, of course!), cycling and walking.

Dad always puts all of himself into his projects. I hope in reading this guide you will enjoy his company even half as much as I have – and still do.

Anna L. Scamans

THE GR10 TRAIL

COAST TO COAST THROUGH THE FRENCH PYRENEES

by

Paul Lucia

2 POLICE SQUARE, MILNTHORPE, CUMBRIA LA7 7PY
www.cicerone.co.uk

ACKNOWLEDGEMENTS

I am very grateful for all the help and encouragement that I have received in the preparation of this guide. In particular, during the summer of 2001 my wife put up with my long absences with patience, light-heartedness and resilience, knowing that I was spending the time in the Pyrenees, which we both hold in great affection. On top of this, she has meticulously checked the manuscript, maps and profiles with me. My daughter offered to write the author profile when she was trying to meet her publisher's deadline for her own book.

Cicerone Press had asked me to prepare the guide as Alan Castle was unable to carry out the much-needed revision to his original *Pyrenean Trail GR10*. Michael Winterton loaned me two old English guides and put me in touch with friends who had walked part of the eastern section. Of those, Malcolm and Sue Fordyce provided useful information, and Lieutenant Colonel Keith Eve kindly gave me a copy of the detailed diary of his own expedition. The knowledge that my son had set his heart on joining me for the difficult Ariège section kept me going when appalling weather almost caused me to abandon the project early on. His companionship and enthusiasm made light of further difficult conditions. Many companions en route added richness to the experience; other trekkers passed on helpful information, while gîte and refuge guardians were always helpful, and some offered transport to nearby villages with food shops. Kev Reynolds, with his extensive knowledge of the Pyrenees, has kindly provided the foreword.

To all these, I owe a deep gratitude, for they have made this book possible.

Advice to Readers

Readers are advised that while every effort is taken by the author to ensure the accuracy of this guidebook, changes can occur which may affect the contents. It is advisable to check locally on transport, accommodation, shops, etc, but even rights of way can be altered. The publisher would welcome notes of any such changes.

CONTENTS

FOREWORD

The 800-odd kilometres of footpath, lane and trackway which link the Atlantic coast with the Mediterranean have created one of the finest long-distance routes in France. GR10, the so-called 'Sentier des Pyrénées', is a walk of epic proportions, routed as it is along the north flank of a magical range of mountains. Unlike its counterpart on the Spanish slope, GR10 actively seeks out a number of villages that lie snug at the foot of the mountains, so the long-distance walker can enjoy both the rugged heartland of the range and the more hospitable landscapes tended by a pastoral community. Some villages, like Aïnhoa in the Basque country, and Lescun below Pic d'Anie, are true gems, while further east the route fights a way across the lonely, seemingly forgotten, country of Haute Ariège. The route winds round the base of Pic du Midi d'Ossau, and on a *variante* crosses a col almost within arm's-reach of the Vignemale's impressive North Face before sneaking below the snout of the longest glacier in the range. The promise of such scenes and contrasts adds a *frisson* of expectation for anyone planning a walk from Hendaye to Banyuls.

Having explored both sides of these mountains over a number of years, Paul Lucia has become something of an authority on – as well as a great enthusiast for – the Pyrenees. That enthusiasm inspired his guide to the GR11 (*Through the Spanish Pyrenees*), first published by Cicerone in 1996, and is the hallmark of his approach to this present guide. It is an enthusiasm we both share with the Victorian pioneer, Charles Packe, who wrote the first English-language guidebook to these mountains in 1862, and who summed up their appeal thus: 'The principal charm of the Pyrenees consists in the unrivalled scenery.'

Anyone who tackles the GR10 with Paul Lucia's book will echo those words and, surely, will join the growing band of activists who in recent years have become hooked on this wonderfully scenic range of mountains.

Kev Reynolds

Pic du Midi d'Ossau

INTRODUCTION

Walkers of all ages and abilities are drawn to the Pyrenees by the combined attractions of a waymarked trail and the availability of accommodation and meals at the end of most days, meaning that lighter loads can be carried. A further advantage is the 'fireside fellowship' particularly enjoyed by the French. However, make no mistake about it: trekking the GR10 coast to coast, with its 49,000m of ascent and descent, vagaries of the weather, navigation difficulties and replenishment of supplies and water to sort out, is a serious undertaking. Nevertheless, anyone properly prepared should not be deterred. A tent is not necessary (except, perhaps, while crossing the Ariège), and very few walkers carry one; if prepared meals can be afforded, carrying cooking kit and large quantities of food can also be avoided.

In this guide the route has been divided into 50 walking days, mostly determined by the availability of lodgings. However, it is not intended that this breakdown should be followed religiously, though the logic of it is inescapable. For 23 days, all the way to Bagnères-de-Luchon, there are adequate lodgings. There is accommodation for a further three days, but the lack of food shops means that

planning for the next 15 days to Mérens-les-Vals must be concluded at Luchon. My observations and suggestions in this respect appear at the beginning of this section in the hope that they may be of some help in managing this part of the walk. Thereafter, from Mérens to the coast, the route passes through excellent walking country with the likelihood of more stable weather and suitable lodgings at the end of each day.

ACCESS

Road: There is no need to give details here as almost every day has road access at some point. Road atlases will show most of the roads, but 1:50,000 IGN maps are needed for the local mountain roads, and there will be lots of new sections not shown even on these.

Air: With very cheap air fares available, flying is a good option. RyanAir fly to Biarritz and Pau in the west and Perpignan in the east. Flights to other airports close by the GR10, such as Lourdes, are usually only available from Paris. Other city airports either side of the Pyrenees require more time and expense to reach the mountains. If flying into Biarritz, the train station is about 3km away, with services to Hendaye. There is also a bus service that stops on the

Sare (Day 2)

N10 as it crosses the route of the GR10. There is a bus shuttle, *la Navette*, from the airport at Perpignan to the town some 5–6km to the south. There is a Youth Hostel in Perpignan, near the main railway station to the west of town. Follow the road north from the station, beside the tracks, turning right at the main junction into avenue de Grande-Bretagne. A few hundred metres later, just before the large police station, turn left and the Youth Hostel is at the end of the turning on the right.

Rail: Eurostar and SNCF have combined return tickets to the main towns north of the mountains. The cheapest fares require that dates are specified and the same town is used for outgoing and return journeys. Local travel can then be done using single tickets. The Metro connects Paris Nord to Montparnasse station, where the French TGV service swiftly

conveys its passengers southwards. Taking the first Eurostar from London to Bordeaux can mean that Hendaye is reached by mid-afternoon and walking commences the very same day! Bear in mind that Bordeaux is in a cheaper fare band than Toulouse. There are ongoing rail services to Hendaye, Bidarray, St-Jean-Pied-de-Port, Bagnères-de-Luchon, Mérens-les-Vals, Bolquère, La Cabanasse and Banyuls-sur-Mer.

Coach: Coach travel, once the economic way to the south of France, has rather been eclipsed by cheap flights or faster rail. Eurolines run services to Bayonne, Pau, Lourdes and Perpignan. The service to Toulouse connects with a small coach to Andorra.

EQUIPMENT

Whatever equipment you decide to take, make it as light as possible. You will need a comfortable rucksack in good condition. There is no compelling reason to take a tent and cooking kit as far as Luchon, and from Mérens to the coast, as adequate accommodation is available each night. However, the cost of lodgings, though individually quite cheap, can mount up significantly over 50 or more days. Only a small saving can be made by using campsites, but a considerable sum by cooking one's own meals, either in the tent or in the gîte. Through the Haute Ariège there are plenty of cabins, but these are not always available for use by walkers and some do not have a water supply; a tent here is a great asset. You should have lightweight boots, preferably waterproof, and three sets of socks. Gaiters are heavy and may not be used much, but stop-tous are most useful as they can do just what their

name implies, and are especially useful for keeping snow out of boots in springtime, and socks dry when walking through wet grass. A pair of lightweight trainers or sandals is more or less essential. Boots are not allowed to be worn in either gîtes or refuges and there is little protection in socks, though refuges tend to supply some form of footwear. As for all mountain areas, a breathable and waterproof outer layer is essential. But nevertheless, shorts are the order of the day, with a pair of trousers for evening and travel wear. Take three sets of underwear, of the quick-drying variety; there will be days when washing cannot be dried. Take three tops, keeping one for evening and travel, since the others will become grubby-looking without machine washing. You will need a warm top, fleece or equivalent for evening use, and you should pack a

Hourquette d'Ossoue variant – Oulettes d'Ossoue

sun hat that really does stop the sun. Gloves might be needed on rare occasions, though I use a dry pair of socks instead. In theory, if using gîtes and refuges, there is no need to carry a sleeping bag – just a sheet – as blankets are provided. In practice, blankets may not be available and some nights will be very cold, so a lightweight bag is essential, and you will need a warmer one if camping. A camping mat will only be necessary if camping, or if using the cabanes of the Ariège. Walking poles cum ski sticks are very popular now, and I can recommend their use. You will need water containers capable of holding several litres of water, plus a personal water bottle carried on the outside of your sack for easy access. A compass and the knowledge of how to use it are essential; maps and guides are dealt with below. Many gîtes and refuges provide kitchen areas for personal meal preparation, and many gîtes have cooking stoves as well. Personal cooking kit is needed if camping and if you want to cook in those places without such provision. Bear in mind that re-sealable gas cylinders are not readily available in the Pyrenees, and that gas cylinders are not allowed on aircraft.

Gourette (Day 14)

FACILITIES LIST

A list of facilities is provided at the end of the book. The heading 'Gîte' refers to gîtes d'étape, and a shop is indicated when some provisions can be purchased, either from an épicerie or sold at the accommodation, if this is a regular feature. Locations in brackets lie a short distance from the main GR10, and crosses in brackets indicate that the facility is unlikely to be open during a coast-to-coast walk (involving a start early in the season). These might be open in July/August, as well as during the skiing season. 'Hotel' means a hotel, auberge or a place where rooms are available. 'Campsite' refers not only to campsites but also to those places where camping is allowed and facilities available.

FITNESS

The enjoyment of walking this trail will be greatly enhanced by prior physical preparation. If you deem that you are out of condition, gradually try to fit in as much walking into your day as possible. Little and often is better than an occasional all-day outing. Start taking a daysack and then your rucksack, eventually loaded well above what you expect to carry. Then, more for psychological reasons than physical, do at least one 30km walk with weight. Have hard weeks and easy weeks to allow your body time to adjust. One great advantage of such gradual preparation is that you may well avoid the dreaded blistered feet. In the Pyrenees, distance is not the overriding factor when assessing the amount of effort required. The total ascent is the yardstick; and, if your knees are not too strong, the total descent has to be considered too.

FOOD SHOPS

Replenishing supplies is sometimes a problem. Mountain folk still living in the villages tend to go by car to the nearest town supermarket. Shops open during the summer can be closed in September for their holidays. The most dramatic closure in recent times has been the épicerie at Fos, as this is at the very start of the Ariège; fortunately the boulangerie is still functioning. It is possible, but never certain, that lunch and trail food can be obtained from gîtes, refuges and bars en route. Information is given in the daily descriptions.

Crags NE of the Hourquette d'Arre (Day 14)

Lescun (Day 12)

GEOGRAPHY

The Pyrenean mountain chain can be said to begin as a rocky promontory on the Atlantic coast of Spain in the south-east corner of the Bay of Biscay, and extends roughly east-south-east some 435km, as the crow flies, to another such headland on the north-west coast of the Mediterranean Sea. The GR10 manages to double this distance and more. It will be noticed from maps that high ground coming from the east passes to the north of that coming from the west, thus forming the valley, Val d'Aran. Fos lies at the mouth of this valley, just inside the French border. From the Atlantic coast, the hills soon rise to La Rhune (900m), below which the first day ends. On the final day to the Mediterranean, Pic Néoulous (1025m) is climbed, and the route passes close to the summit of Pic de

Sailfort (981m). The highest pass on the main route is the Col de la Madamète (2509m), which is passed on the 19th day. The three-day extension via the Hourquette d'Ossoue rises to 2734m.

GÎTES D'ÉTAPE

These are not to be confused with 'gîtes de France', which are holiday lettings. I refer to the gîtes d'étape in this guide as 'gîtes'. The gîtes d'étape, at the very basic, provide dormitory accommodation, a kitchen and dining area, toilet facilities including showers, and are near or in villages or hamlets. Many also provide a half-board service and will have some basic provisions, but they do like to have advance warning of meals required. The Rando'Plume gives a higher standard of accommodation, possibly in a better building, often in smaller rooms, always offering half-board and other services. These are, of course, a little more expensive. Many gîtes can be accessed by car, so it is always advisable to book in advance. Obtain, at the earliest opportunity, the leaflet listing the current gîtes and refuges along the GR10, stocked by many gîtes and produced by CIMES-Pyrénées. Their address and telephone number are on the IGN Randonnées Pyrénéenes maps. The telephone numbers of those gîtes not included in the 2001–2002 pamphlet are given in the text.

GUIDEBOOKS

The Fédération Française de la Randonnée Pédestre has produced a guide to the GR10 in French comprising four volumes. They are especially useful for the reproduced IGN maps with the route indicated thereon, though not always correctly. *Trekking the Pyrenees* by Douglas Streatfeild-James contains much useful information, and especially helpful are the town diagrams, indicating the location of gîtes, hotels, etc, together with telephone numbers. He doesn't follow the whole course of the GR10, but describes a most practical way of tackling it – perhaps the way it ought to be.

Walks and Climbs in the Pyrenees by Kev Reynolds (Cicerone Press) is an excellent introduction to the Pyrenees with a large selection of itineraries, describing access to and walks in the most delectable parts of the high mountains. It also has a section on the High Route, the Haute Randonnée Pyrénéenne (HRP).

INSURANCE

It is important to check that your travel insurance covers trekking in the

Vignemale (Hourquette d'Ossoue variant)

Pyrenees as not all do, and that helicopter rescue is covered.

MAPS

The whole route is covered by the IGN 1:50,000 Carte de Randonnée series maps. Numbers 1 to 8, 10 and 11 are required. There are also 1:25,000 maps, but these would be extremely expensive to buy for complete coverage of the route and very heavy to carry. For much the same price as a set of 1:50,000 maps, one can purchase the four volumes of the French guide which contain relevant parts of the 1:50,000 set. These are adequate, but mean that it is often impossible to identify distant mountains without a larger sheet.

MOUNTAIN HUTS

These are referred to, on maps and in guides, as refuges, or chalet-hôtels if individual rooms are available. All meals are taken communally. Manned mountain huts are situated high in the mountains beside long-distance trails. Camping is usually allowed nearby and a full meals service provided. Access to the unisex dormitories is not normally permitted until the evening. Some carry gas and other supplies.

There are also unstaffed huts called refuges or cabanes on maps. The condition of these can vary greatly, and they are often used by herdsmen and sometimes cattle. The best afford comfortable shelter, fire, mattresses and a good clean water supply, but they are often full in the height of summer.

MOUNTAIN RESCUE

The telephone numbers for local emergency assistance are to be found beside the map key on the IGN

Morning above Gave de Labat (Day 16)

trekking maps. Whoever goes for assistance must have a clear and accurately marked map showing the position of the person(s) in need of rescue. Helicopters are directed by both arms being raised above the head.

PROFILES

A profile, with the vertical scale enlarged, is provided in the text for each day.

SKETCH MAPS

A map key is included at the end of the Introduction to show the meaning of the various symbols used. The bold letters in boxes, indicating some of the facilities available, have been drawn on the maps even if they are likely to be closed in May or June. Not everyone using this guide will be walking the whole route and needing to start in June. Please refer to the Facilities List at the end of the book and daily descriptions for more information. It is not intended that these maps should be used instead of the proper IGN ones but as a supplement. They do show most junctions and whether the route is on path, track or road. The 1:50,000 official maps do not give as much detail. The heights given are either official or estimated from maps, and differ from these only when I have noticed obvious errors, as at Planès (where the spot height refers to the high part of the village, whereas the gîte is in the lower part). The maps have been drawn with the French grid as the north–south line. The magnetic north differs little from this (2002). Checks against map data should be made.

SNOW

As the GR10 traverses the northern slopes of the range snow can be encountered on the high passes long into summer. This forces a later start for the coast-to-coast walker, to avoid problems during for the first 13 days. The Hourquette d'Arrre at 2465m presents the main difficulty. The condition of the snow here can usually be ascertained from other walkers coming from the east, and from the lady who runs the Gabas refuge.

TIMINGS

There is much controversy about guide timings in general. These are, of course, only an indicator, but I find that consistency is more important than the times being set at my own particular pace. For example, on Day 33 my son and I arrived at the water channel, and the French guide stated 45 minutes from there to Auzat. In spite of the fact that we had only been taking about 70 per cent of the guide times, we took 1 hour 14 minutes to reach the bar at Auzat at a fast march! The times given in this guide are the estimated walking time only. An allowance for pauses and stops needs to be added. No account is taken of adverse weather conditions: rain, mist, storms or

View back to Coll de Coma d'Anyell (Day 40)

exceptional heat will obviously affect one's performance. Usually this means about 20–30 per cent extra has to be added to indicate the likely time from start to finish (in fine weather). The times indicated are cumulative for each day, and represent the approximate time needed by a reasonably fit person carrying 17kg. These have been calculated by comparing the times of three other guides with my own timing, allowing for the fact that sometimes I was carrying 13kg and at others 17–18kg. All time taken for lunch breaks, photos, note taking and locating the route were deducted (with the exclusion of short rest stops on steep climbs: these were considered part of the walking time). Someone in good

condition should find these times generous. For the record, camping kit was carried from Luz-St-Sauveur to Mérens-les-Vals, but for the coastal sections either side of this no such equipment was taken.

WATER

Cattle are grazed at high altitudes during the summer, and can be found at unbelievable heights. This makes all surface water suspect and it is better to treat it before use. Springs and piped water tend to be quite pure, though investigation of piped supply is worthwhile. As I use 2.5l Platypus bottles, Micropur MT 5 tablets are ideal for sterilisation, using half a tablet per bottle. These tablets are tasteless, do not seem to have any ill effects, and even seem to work on brown-coloured water. I have not been aware of any poor water quality from taps in lodgings. It is wise, especially in hot weather, to start the day with a plentiful supply.

IGN 1:50,000 maps was sometimes different to that on the ground, particularly during Days 36 to 38, and 47, of this guide. Very occasionally signposts and noticeboards had been vandalised.

WAYMARKING AND NAVIGATION

The white-and-red stripes of a GR are used, with a white change-of-direction arrow added as appropriate. The very useful wrong-direction red-and-white cross is used on paths, tracks and roads not to be followed. There are regular signposts noting location, height and times to other places. During 2001 the waymarking was very good. However, the route indicated in the French guides and on

WEATHER

Expect there to be early morning mists, low cloud and periods of rain in the early part of the route. Variable weather conditions can persist right through to the Ariège, but the final week enjoys more of a Mediterranean climate and can be very hot in summer. Storms can appear, as if from nowhere. Coping with the changing weather is the most challenging aspect of the walk.

Early morning mist at Seix (Day 30)

WILD CAMPING

While in France it is important to recognise the difference between 'camping' and 'the bivouac'. My understanding, and the English dictionary definition, of bivouac are the passing of the night in the open as opposed to being under cover. In France bivouac also implies an overnight stop in a small mountain tent, which can mean that while no camping is allowed, the bivouac is accepted. However, it is made clear that the only bivouac site while passing through the Réserve Naturelle de Néouvielle is below the Aubert lake. Suitable places to camp are marked on the sketch maps when these were noticed, but overnight stops can be made in so many other places that anyone wanting to camp should not be deterred.

NOTES ON USING THIS GUIDE

The daily stages are sequentially numbered and give a summary of the estimated distance, height gain and loss, and the walking time required. They are also provided with a profile. All measurements are metric. The bold figures in blue at the start of each paragraph in the text indicate the accumulative time for that particular day. The word 'road' in the text refers to a tarmac or concrete surfaced road. Sometimes 'lane' is used just as another word for a narrow road. 'Track' means a wide dirt, gravel, farm or grassy route that can be used by vehicles. 'Path' refers to those trails that only take foot traffic (human and animal), and perhaps the occasional mountain bike. General compass directions given as N (north), ESE (east-south-east), and so on, are to assist in choosing the correct route especially where there appears to be a choice. Left and right, in relation to a stream or valley, refer to the true left or right, that is, when looking down the flow. The High Level Route is referred to as HRP both in the text and on the sketch maps. Though the GR10 route is adequately waymarked, I have presented a detailed route description, for at numerous junctions the way is unclear as confirming marks take some time to appear. It is only too easy to miss change-of-direction and no-way marks while peering at a map or guide, or talking with a companion. Most walkers will find themselves very tired at times, and it is hoped that this guide will assist in reducing the extra work and time spent in trying to confirm the way. It is also hoped that such detail will encourage less experienced walkers to embark on this great trek. The sketch maps are also designed to assist by showing the route junctions where scale allows.

NB. Please note that some refuges only open in mid-June and can close in early September.

MAP KEY

------------ GR10

Motorway

Main Road

Minor road

Piste

Path

National border

River or Stream

Railway line

Lakes

Contour heights are represented by shading starting at 300m and then at 500m intervals. Each map starts with the lowest height band without shading.

⚟ Wild Campsite

▲ Campsite location

W Water point

△ Trig. point

■ Notable building

GHRSTBReCCa.   Gite, Hotel, Restaurant, Shop, Telephone, Bank, Refuge, Camping site, Cabin

ROUTE SUMMARY

DAY	STAGE	HEIGHT GAIN (METRES)	HEIGHT LOSS (METRES)	TIME	DIST. (KM)	ACC. DIST. (KM)
1	Hendaye – Olhette	1004	924	6hrs 15mins	20.5	20.5
2	Olhette – Ainhoa	636	596	5hrs 40mins	21.5	42.0
3	Ainhoa – Bidarray	766	736	6hrs 20mins	20.3	62.3
4	Bidarray – St-Étienne-de-Baïgorry	1260	1248	7hrs 25mins	15.7	78.0
5	St-Étienne-de-Baïgorry – St-Jean-Pied-de-Port	859	864	6hrs 15mins	20.0	98.0
6	St-Jean-Pied-de-Port – Estérençuby	489	415	3hrs 25mins	13.1	111.1
7	Estérençuby – Col Bagargiak	1840	744	7hrs 15mins	24.0	135.1
8	Col Bagargiak – Logibar	424	1376	5hrs 40mins	16.7	151.8
9	Logibar – St-Engrâce	1187	932	6hrs 00mins	23.0	174.8
10	St-Engrâce – Arette-la-Pierre-St-Martin	1185	165	4hrs 30mins	12.3	187.1
11	Arette-la Pierre-St-Martin – Lescun	340	1090	5hrs 00mins	15.1	202.2
12	Lescun – Estaut	789	1092	5hrs 15mins	16.3	218.5
13	Estaut – Gabas	1588	1158	7hrs 20mins	24.7	243.2
14	Gabas – Gourette	1468	1149	8hrs 25mins	22.5	265.6
15	Gourette – Arrens-Marsous	640	1108	4hrs 30mins	14.0	279.7
16	Arrens-Marsous – Cauterets	1574	1539	9hrs 15mins	27.1	306.8
17	Cauterets – Luz-St-Sauveur	1248	1441	7hrs 00mins	22.0	328.8
18	Luz-St-Sauveur – Barèges	832	312	3hrs 50mins	12.1	340.9
19	Barèges – Chalet-Hôtel Lac de l'Oule	1309	728	7hrs 50mins	22.7	363.6
20	Chalet-Hôtel Lac de l'Oule – Vielle-Aure	394	1415	4hrs 50mins	16.3	379.9
21	Vielle-Aure – Germ	1165	626	4hrs 30mins	13.0	392.9
22	Germ – Lac d'Oô	1176	1011	5hrs 45mins	15.7	408.6
23	Lac d'Oô – Bagnères-de-Luchon	1003	1857	6hrs 50mins	18.5	427.1
24	Bagnères-de-Luchon – Fos	1524	1630	9hrs 40mins	27.0	454.1
25	Fos – Réf. de l'Étang d'Araing	1651	245	6hrs 40mins	17.9	472.0
26	Réf. de l'Étang d'Araing – Eylie-d'en-Haut	310	1270	3hrs 20mins	7.3	479.3
27	Eylie-d'en-Haut – Cabane de Besset	1296	792	5hrs 50mins	11.5	490.8

DAY	STAGE	HEIGHT GAIN (METRES)	HEIGHT LOSS (METRES)	TIME	DIST. (KM)	ACC. DIST. (KM)
28	Cabane de Besset – Étang d'Ayès	1402	1202	7hrs 15mins	14.5	505.3
29	Étang d'Ayès – Aunac	497	1425	6hrs 10mins	19.6	524.9
30	Aunac – Rouze	1696	1532	9hrs 25mins	28.4	553.3
31	Rouze – St-Lizier-d'Ustou	616	806	2hrs 50mins	7.1	560.4
32	St-Lizier-d'Ustou – Aulus-les-Bains	1361	1351	8hrs 40mins	22.5	582.9
33	Aulus-les-Bains – Mounicou	1330	993	7hrs 55mins	22.3	605.2
34	Mounicou – Goulier	1372	1349	7hrs 45mins	25.3	630.5
35	Goulier – Siguer	439	809	4hrs 00mins	13.2	643.7
36	Siguer – Ref. de Clarans	1657	1297	8hrs 55mins	18.7	662.4
37	Ref. de Clarans – Ref. du Rulhe	1626	541	8hrs 00mins	18.0	680.4
38	Ref. du Rulhe – Mérens-les-Vals	437	1572	5hrs 00mins	12.6	693.0
39	Mérens-les-Vals – Ref. des Bésines	1367	313	4hrs 20mins	9.5	702.5
40	Ref. des Bésines – Ref. des Bouillouses	602	696	5hrs 50mins	18.0	720.5
41	Ref. des Bouillouses – Planès	167	677	4hrs 35mins	18.2	738.7
42	Planès – Ref. du Ras de la Carança	1168	837	5hrs 15mins	14.8	753.5
43	Ref. du Ras de la Carança – Mantet	591	887	4hrs 00mins	11.0	764.5
44	Mantet – Ref. de Mariailles	1030	847	5hrs 05mins	14.5	779.0
45	Ref. de Mariailles – Chalet-Hôtel des Cortalets	990	558	5hrs 40mins	17.3	796.3
46	Chalet-Hôtel des Cortalets – Mines de Batère	273	923	4hrs 00mins	16.8	813.1
47	Mines de Batère – Moulin de la Palette	629	1468	5hrs 30mins	20.6	833.7
48	Moulin de la Palette – Las Illas	902	1013	7hrs 05mins	21.0	854.7
49	Las Illas – Chalet de l'Albère	959	573	5hrs 50mins	24.8	879.5
50	Chalet de l'Albère – Banyuls-sur-Mer	646	1582	6hrs 35mins	24.2	903.7
TOTALS		49714	49714	305hrs 05mins	903.7	903.7

Pont de Pierres (Day 33)

Day 1: Hendaye to Olhette

Distance:	20.5km (12.7 miles)
Height gain:	1004m
Height loss:	924m
Time:	6hrs 15mins
Maps:	IGN Carte de Randonnées No. 1

0.00 Hendaye. The GR10 starts at the Casino at Hendaye Plage. Turn your back on the Atlantic and go along Boulevard du Général Leclerc, SSE, to a square where a half-right turn is taken along Rue des Citronniers to the road by the bay. Turn left and follow the road. *One can follow the promenade beside the bay, which is nicer, turning left to pass under the bridge to a small square.* The road turns away from the bay to join with a road coming directly from the Casino. Bear right and about 300m later, at the top of the rise and about 50m from a bridge, turn left down Rue de Belcenia to the small square. Do not go straight on and under the railway

This long and varied trek starts with a gentle stroll through Hendaye Plage and pleasantly along the Bay of Chingoudy before climbing a small hill, passing the N10 and A63 roads. Then the climbing begins. This sets the pattern for many days: a climb during the morning with a descent during the afternoon. It provides a routine to which coast-to-coast walkers will become quite accustomed.

Hendaye Plage

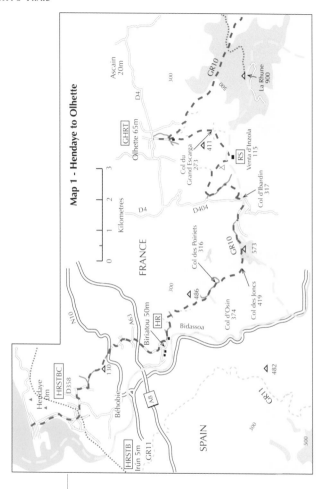

Map 1 - Hendaye to Olhette

bridge. Go through the arch on the left to Rue Parcheteguia and then left again up Rue Subornea, passing the railway by a small underpass. Climb the road on the other side to the D358. Continue up the D358 for 150m and then bear right up Rue Errondenia, as the main road bears left. At the top, at a T-junction, turn right along a track for about 300m to a junction. Turn left, and almost immediately take the right fork, following the track, E, to the left side of Pt 130 to join with the N10. Turn left for 100m, then turn right, SE, down a short driveway, then track, and then path. Follow the path to a small road that soon descends towards the SE. Look out for a left turn that leads steeply down to another road. Opposite and slightly to the right is a narrow road. Take this and follow it through a small tunnel under the motorway. Climb the road, very steeply at first, to a house, where a sign and marks indicate a left turn. *If lodgings are required, try at the house, or continue along the road as it turns back right to...*

2.00 Biriatou, 50m. Take the short spur road by the house and follow the track, and in a few minutes turn sharp left, and left again along a path. This climbs E towards the hill ahead and crosses a track. Avoiding paths turning left. The trail turns to the SSE, beneath the rocks, to reach...

3.05 Col d'Osin, 374m. A wide track joins from the left that is followed SE down to Col des Poiriets (316m). The track soon turns to the N and a path continues SE to Col des Joncs (419m). There is a sharp left, then right, and then the path contours the north of Mandalé, Pt 573 on the sketch map. This joins a track that goes down to a road and the border with Spain. Go steeply down the road through the buildings (possibility of refreshments), to...

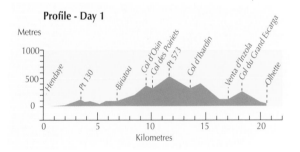

Profile - Day 1

4.10 Col d'Ibardin, 317m. Take the D404 north for a few metres, and at a signpost take the track on the right. Shortly after take a right fork and then, at a gate, right again, climbing a path steeply to a track that descends NW. Just before this joins the D404, turn off right and follow a path, E, down the north side of the valley. About 1km later, turn right, SE, along the remains of an ancient paved track beside a stream. This leads into Spain and…

5.15 Venta d'Inzola, 115m. *Refreshments and some provisions may be obtained, but no accommodation.* Cross the footbridge, about 20m N of the Venta, first taking the right turning, SE, and follow the path N and then NE. This climbs to the Col du Grand Escarga (273m) and a five-way junction of paths. Take the one going NNE, and 10 to 15mins later a left fork that leads to, at the road head, the gîte d'étape at…

6.15 Olhette, 65m (gîte, 80m). *There is an hotel/restaurant and public telephone 450m down the road.*

Day 2: Olhette to Ainhoa

Distance:	21.5km (13.4 miles)
Height gain:	636m
Height loss:	596m
Time:	5hrs 40mins
Maps:	IGN Carte de Randonnées No. 1

La Rhune is a substantial summit at 900m, but it is passed on the north-east ridge at the Col des Trois Fontaines. Care needed here in misty conditions.

0.00 Olhette gîte, 80m. Go down the road spur from the gîte, cross the stream and climb the path on the other side. Within the next 15mins take two left turns to the E, and then another NE, before turning SE. Avoid a turn to the right a little later. Climb to...

1.10 Col des Trois Fontaines, 563m. *In mist, do not bear right, S, which continues up to the summit of La Rhune.* At the pass, pick up the path going E, starting slightly to

Change of direction and crags below La Rhune

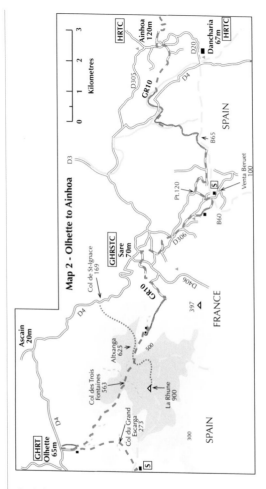

Map 2 - Olhette to Ainhoa

the left. Bear right, SE, at the next junction, cross the rack-railway line and go down the left side of the valley ahead. As the path reaches a ruined farm with a field on the right soon look for a sharp right turn a little further on. From the farm, cross a small stream, and at the next ruin, turn sharp right down to the stream again. Climb the other side to a farm track, turn left and follow it all the way down to a road. Follow the road, left, and as it turns down right, bear left to locate a path that is followed to another road. Go down the road, cross the road in the valley and climb the road ahead into...

2.40 Sare, 70m. *Hotels, shops and a campsite with gîte (about 1.5km SSW of Sare). NB: Sare and Ainhoa are very popular tourist destinations. Booking in advance is recommended. Re-provision here as there is little likelihood at Ainhoa.* The GR turns right, SSE, at the top of the steep road section just before Sare centre. Go down the paved way, over the bridge and up the steps to a road. Turn left and follow left past a junction. A few minutes later, take the narrow path right, SSE, and follow down to another road, the D306. Turn right and follow for 500m. Turn left along a narrow road, keeping left at a fork, to the Camping Tellechea, which only opens during July and August. Just past the campsite take the narrow lane on the right, SSW. Shortly, turn left into the farmyard and right behind the buildings. Follow the farm track S, past the barrier, to waymarks. Continue to a narrow road that is followed to Venta Berouet, with a large car parking area. *Café and toilets may be useful.* Follow the road north, ignore the turn right, and after about 200m take the right fork. This route avoids private property on the border. At the T-junction Pt 120, turn right and follow the lane back to the border again. Turn

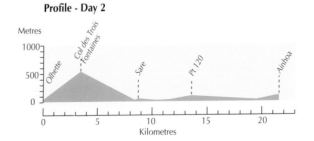

Profile - Day 2

35

left at the next junction, now E, and follow this road until waymarks direct along a track on the left, ENE. This track changes direction past border stones but makes its way generally NNE. After 1km or so, marks lead off to the left on a path beside the river. This returns to the track and crosses it as it passes through a picnic area, then joins the track again. Follow this, ESE, to the bridge on the left. Cross the bridge and road, D4, following the track around to the E. After a few minutes this becomes a path leading to a road that is followed into...

5.40 Ainhoa, 120m. *The gîte has now closed but there are several hotels. Camping Harazpy is close by, in the field by the primary school: ask at the mairie. If accommodation is all taken, there is a hotel and campsite at Dancharia, 2km S, on the border.*

Day 3: Ainhoa to Bidarray

Distance:	20.3km (12.6 miles)
Height gain:	766m
Height loss:	736m
Time:	6hrs 20mins
Maps:	IGN Carte de Randonnées No. 1

No real problems with navigation today, and the chance of a good lunch near the halfway mark. Care is needed to pick the correct trail at Col de Méhatché, but even more so when descending the ravine after Pt 676. Those used to steep, loose and exposed descents will not be troubled, but anyone who dislikes such places will have to go very carefully. Wet conditions will make this fairly dangerous for all. The exposure continues for a long way, but the upper steepest part soon eases.

Traverse below Point 676

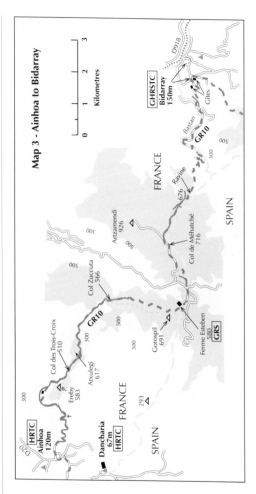

Map 3 - Ainhoa to Bidarray

0.00 Ainhoa, 120m. From the centre of the village, opposite the church, take the narrow road E, with a sign to the Argi Eder hotel and GR timings. Before long the road becomes a wide track, climbing first to la Chapelle de l'Aubépine and then passing around the north of

Ereby. A path is taken ESE, which is a short cut across a loop of the track that goes past a farm building before joining the track again. Follow the track to…

1.10 Col des Trois Croix, 510m. Continue on the track, passing Atxulegi on the south side, and follow all the way to…

2.05 Col Zuccuta, 566m. Follow the track S, which becomes a path after about 10mins. *There is a higher trail on the ridge to the W that involves more climbing.* The trail leads to…

2.45 Ferme Esteben, 580m. *There is a gîte here with restaurant and some supplies available at the bar.* Cross the farmyard and take the road going down, E, to the Col de Veaux (540m). Take the track opposite that climbs N. After a few minutes, leave the track for a path on the right that leads to the road, which is followed to…

3.25 Col de Méhatché, 716m. A broad path goes E, soon becoming a rough track turning SE. Ignore paths going down to the S. Continue straight on past a junction and look out for a path in the grass, going back, on the right. This is the start of the steep descent of the ravine near to…

3.55 Pt 676 on the map. *The Iparla ridge can be seen to the SE.* Follow the narrow path and much later, above and just past a farm, turn right down to the road. Turn left and follow the road down. *A short cut, shown on maps, does not seem to exist now. Anyway, the road is steep enough.* At the valley bottom, cross the River

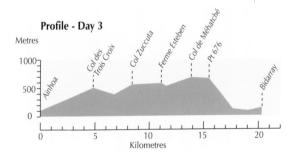

Bastan and follow the road N and then E, beside the river. Where the road crosses the river by a stone bridge, turn right, climbing steeply through the undergrowth, immediately crossing a wide dirt track. Continue climbing to a clear path going NE. This leads to a narrow road that passes the gîte (a cottage seen on the left), but it is necessary to continue up to the main gîte, on the corner, on the right, in order to book.

6.20 Bidarray gîte, 150m. *Gîte, hotel, restaurant and shop. There is a lower part to the town, by the river, that boasts more hotels and the railway station. About 1km S from here is Camping Errekaldia.*

Day 4: Bidarray to St-Étienne-de-Baïgorry

Distance:	15.7km (9.8 miles)
Height gain:	1260m
Height loss:	1248m
Time:	7hrs 25mins
Maps:	IGN Carte de Randonnées No. 1

0.00 Bidarray gîte, 150m. Take the road S, beside the upper gîte, and bear right at the fork. Go right again through farm buildings, then left to a path that climbs towards the SW. This eventually scrambles around the right of some rocks; it is important not to follow the trail seen ahead, traversing the hillside to the right. Avoid another path right, and follow marks that lead to the eastern side of the ridge and back to the ridge again later. At another grassy area fork right, following the path climbing to the skyline. Continue to a summit and then on to...

This is the first really hard day, best done in fine weather. The long border ridge of Crête d'Iparla is hard work but gives excellent views, starting with an exposed but safe traverse of the initial crags. Water can be replenished at Col d'Harrieta, but don't rely on it.

Iparla ridge (Col d'Harrieta at centre)

41

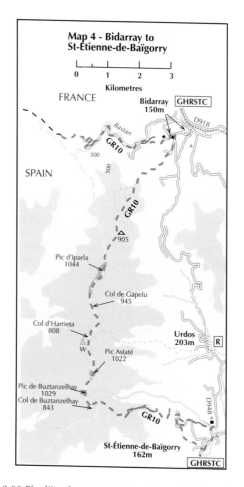

**Map 4 - Bidarray to
St-Étienne-de-Baïgorry**

3.00 Pic d'Iparla, 1044m. Follow the undulating ridge, past Col de Gapelu, to the steep descent to...
4.05 Col d'Harrieta, 808m. *Surprisingly, a beech wood covers the slope ahead. Camping is also possible here. There is a water source about 4mins' level walk to the right. If the weather is bad and you have had enough,*

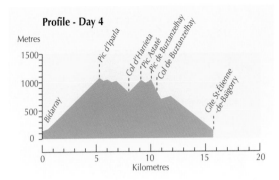

the path down E from the col goes to Urdos. Climb the very steep slope ahead to eventually reach the summits of Astaté (1022m) and Buztanzelhay (1029m). Search to the right to find the trail descending to...

5.25 Col de Buztanzelhay, 843m. Descend NE by a small stream for a short distance and then take the path gently climbing to the ridge on the right. This meets a track; turn left, NNE, and 10mins or so later take the right fork, crossing to the S side of the ridge. A few more minutes later leave the track for a path right, SE. A path soon leaves the ridge to the left. Soon turn right, SSE, as the path meets a track. Turn right at the road and follow down to a sharp right turn. *There is supposed to be a short cut across the loop of the road but I did not see it. There is also a forest track from the southern bend of the road that goes directly to town.* At the bend continue down the road for the town centre or take the track, ESE, with the sign, 'Camping à la ferme'. This leads directly to a road that leads to the main D948. Turn left, and the gîte is found a short way up the road at...

7.25 St-Étienne-de-Baïgorry, 162m. *Hotels, restaurants, shops and camping beside the gîte. No meals available at the gîte but a restaurant is nearby. There is a super-market and another campsite across the bridge on the left on the way into town from the gîte.*

Day 5: *St-Étienne-de-Baïgorry to St-Jean-Pied-de-Port*

Mostly road and track walking today, with a pleasant trail over the top of Monhoa.

Distance:	20km (12.4 miles)
Height gain:	859m
Height loss:	864m
Time:	6hrs 15mins
Maps:	IGN Carte de Randonnées No. 1

Overlooking St-Étienne

0.00 St-Etienne-de-Baïgorry, 162m. From the gîte, go down to the town centre, cross the river and take the lane, on the left, E, beside the police station. Pass under the railway line and turn right. Bear right at the next fork, S, and several minutes later take a track also going S. Ignore a path that goes off left but almost immediately take to another, also on the left. This leads to another track that goes to a road. Ignore the various turnings shown on the sketch map. Turn right onto the road, S.

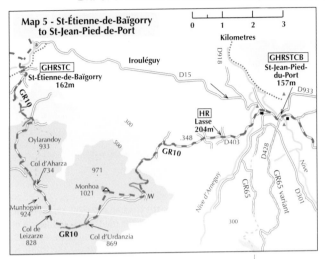

This used to be a dirt track but has recently been surfaced. A few minutes later, at a junction, turn right, SW, continuing along the road. About 2km later, avoid a turning on the right and another on the left, continuing to...

2.15 Col d'Aharza, 734m. *The last 200m to the pass were unsurfaced, but I expect that the work will now have been completed.* Take the road, slightly W of S, for about 1km and then a path, S. This turns E. Ignore a path left and continue to a track that leads to…

3.10 Col d'Urdanzia, 869m. Go up the road ahead and after a few hundred metres turn left up the clear path to…

3.45 Monhoa, 1021m. Follow the trail E and down to cross a loop of the road to where there is a water tap on one of two water troughs. Take the path below the track, NW, and follow to the track some 500m later. Turn right, E, going down the track, all the way to the road. *This track has been engineered over parts of the old GR10 path. Some small sections are still traceable and can be used as short cuts.*

Profile - Day 5

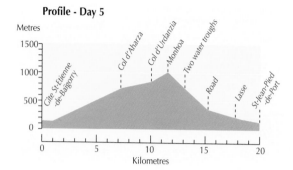

5.10 **The road.** Take the road N and soon a track on the right, S, to join with another road that is followed to a junction. Take the road E to…

5.45 **Lasse, 204m.** *There is a hotel/bar here.* Continue E, along the road to…

6.15 **St-Jean-Pied-de-Port, 157m.** *The first hotel is by the fronton and the busy gîte is a little way along the D918, on the right. All services are in the town, including the railway.*

Day 6: St-Jean-Pied-de-Port to Estérençuby

Distance:	13.1km (8.1 miles)
Height gain:	489m
Height loss:	415m
Time:	3hrs 25mins
Maps:	IGN Carte de Randonnées No. 2

Pleasant countryside and an easy day, which is just as well, as Day 7 is very tiring. There is a small shop at Col Bagargiak but no others until Lescun, unless the variant is used from Col Bagargiak; but lodgings and meals are available.

0.00 St-Jean-Pied-de-Port, 157m. From the gîte, go SE along the D918 to the bridge, seen on the left, but do not cross it. Continue ahead on the S side of the Nive in order to cross the next bridge upstream. Follow the cobbled lane up to and past the castle, through the town gate, and at the junction ahead turn right and follow the D401 SSE. About 1km later, take the road right, SSW, and then a path on the left. Very soon it joins a track; take the right fork that passes to the E of Pt 299 at about 280m. This becomes a road just before a crossroads at...
0.50 Caro, 246m. Go straight across and pass around the church to the E and then S. At the five-way crossing, take the second on the left, signposted to Estérençuby. Turn right, S, at the next junction and after 500–600m

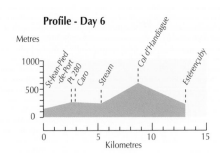

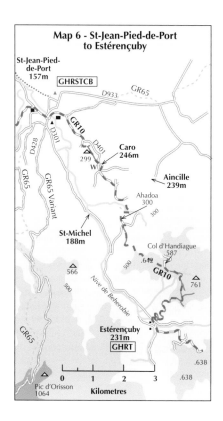

**Map 6 - St-Jean-Pied-de-Port
to Estérençuby**

St-Jean-Pied-de-Port
157m

GHRSTCB

GR65

D933

GR10

D428

D301

D401

Caro
246m

299

W

Aincille
239m

Ahadoa
300

300

St-Michel
188m

GR65

GR65 Variant

Col d'Handiague
587

.642

GR10

566

761

500

Nive de Béhérobie

500

Estérençuby
231m

GHRT

.638

0 1 2 3

Pic d'Orisson
1064

.638

Kilometres

look for a muddy cattle track off right. Pass the gate and later the hurdle to a stream and junction. Cross the stream, ignore a path ahead, turn right and fork left, SW, at the next junction. Follow the path to the road at Ahadoa (300m). Take the track on the other side of the road, S, and pass the gate. Where the track ends, climb left, E, across grass, with a fence on the left, to locate the path more clearly. It turns towards the SE and continues on the E side of the ridge, crossing two stiles. At the second, go straight on, turning left down to the road and signpost at...

2.25 Col d'Handiague, 587m. Turn right and the road soon becomes a wide track that is followed, avoiding all turns to the left, down to…

3.25 Estérençuby, 231m. *There are two hotels and a gîte for accommodation. Hôtel Larramendy Andreinia runs the gîte and provides meals.*

Estérençuby

Day 7: Estérençuby to Col Bagargiak (Chalets d'Irati)

Distance:	24km (14.9 miles)
Height gain:	1840m
Height loss:	744m
Time:	7hrs 15mins
Maps:	IGN Carte de Randonnées No. 2

Fortunately today's 1840m of ascent is split into five separate climbs. Water can be replenished, and cheese and honey purchased, at the small farmhouse that lies below the road to Col d'Irau. Water is also available in the popular Iratiko valley.

0.00 Estérençuby, 231m. Climb the steep lane past the church and follow the road ignoring turnings left and right until, after about 2km, at a left bend, take the track SSE that soon becomes a path. This joins another road that is followed E, ignoring a track right and road, also off right. Ignore a track and another road off left, and an access road left and a crossing track. Pass two more roads to the right and a track left. Then look out for a path on the left, and take the one which leads S at first. This soon crosses the road, then joins it again, going S, to take a track to the right, SSW. In 3–4mins this comes to a five-way junction of tracks, not shown on the sketch map due to the scale. Take the second left, SE,

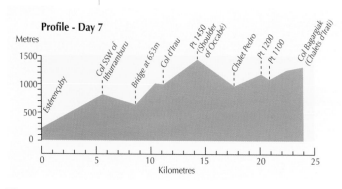

Profile - Day 7

Gîte at Chalets d'Irati after first winter snow

to immediately arrive at a road junction. Take the road, S, that soon becomes a wide track and…

1.55 Col d'Ithurramburu, 820m. Follow the track as it serpentines down E of the Arthe ridge. Around 3km later, after a bridge at 653m, at a right-hand bend, climb steeply up a path on the right, S at first. This leads to the road from Estérençuby, which is followed E. *Water tap at farm below, that also sells cheese and honey.* At the junction with another road, near to a chalet, is…

3.30 Col d'Irau, 1008. Turn right for a few metres and then go left, steeply, up the path, S. At a stone GR10 marker, it joins a track going E. Follow this as it passes beneath the summit of Occabé, seen above and to the right, avoiding turns left then right. Beyond the summit, avoid turns right, then left, and follow steeply down to…

5.15 Chalet Pedro, 990m. *I understand that there is a four-bed room available here, though early booking almost certainly would be required (Tel:*

05.59.28.55.98, fax: 05.59.28.74.43). Turn left, N, along the road, passing first an unmanned refuge, then the picnic/camping area, and then a bar/restaurant set back from the road on the left. *The D301 from Col*

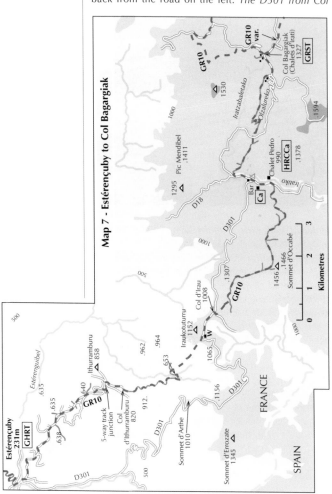

Map 7 - Estérençuby to Col Bagargiak

Estérençuby valley

d'Irau also joins here. Soon leave the road for another on the right that goes to Col Bagargiak. About 100m later turn right and climb a track between fences. Avoid the turning left and a path right. Continue climbing to about 1200m, and then descend to reach the road again at 1100m. Cross the road, pass over an earth dam and take the track S, at first, then climbing zigzags to the E. The track arrives at the road again; the two buildings to the right are no longer used as gîtes for GR10 walkers. Take the road 700m E to the office at…

7.15 Col Bagargiak, 1327m. *There is a new and excellent gîte, with overflow building nearby with meals at the restaurant, on the other side of the track beside the office. There is also a small shop in the restaurant.*

Day 8: Col Bagargiak (Chalets d'Irati) to Logibar

Distance:	16.7km (10.4 miles)
Height gain:	424m
Height loss:	1376m
Time:	5hrs 40mins
Maps:	IGN Carte de Randonnées No. 2

Some relief for the climbing muscles today. If the weather is bad it might be a good idea to take the unmarked shorter but steeper variant down to Larrau, shown on the IGN map and indicated on the sketch map. There is a shop at Larrau as well as hotels and a camp-site, but no gîte. However, the GR10 goes north for a while before turning east and down to Logibar. Route finding can be a bit tricky but, hopefully, the details below will make it easy.

0.00 Col Bagargiak (Chalets d'Irati), 1327m. Take the road that goes down NE, on the E side of the restaurant. About 10mins later, at a right bend in the road, go left, WNW along a track, for a short way, before turning to the right on a path, N. Soon, ignore a path on the right and follow the trail as it gently climbs to the NNW. Keep a sharp look out for the path that turns right to reach the pass a short distance up on the right. *This might be difficult to locate in thick mist.*

0.55 Col at 1423m. Take the delightful path that descends E, then NE, to some shooting booths and the E side of the grassy ridge. At the booth above the road, turn right, SE, and go down steeply to join it. Turn right and follow for 1km to where a wide track goes left towards the ridge ahead and more shooting booths. As the track turns down sharply to the left, turn **right** and look over the edge to see a path contouring the S side of that ridge. I believe that the change-of-direction mark indicates a left turn. Follow marks to go along this trail and not along the ridge. At a junction above a cabin, go down right, SE, past the cabin where water is available. The path comes to a track that curves round the head of a valley above a farm, turning S, to the farm…

2.20 Cayolar Mendikotziague, 980m. Take the path, SE, that turns E, and avoid paths left then right. Fifteen minutes after this last junction the trail turns sharp left to join a parallel path going NNE. Follow this round to

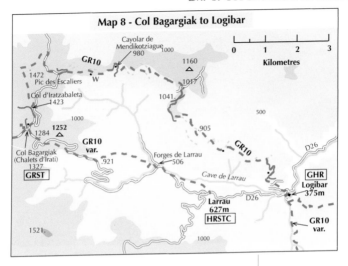

Map 8 - Col Bagargiak to Logibar

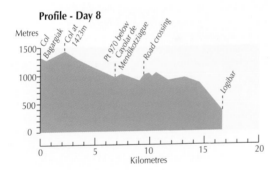

the S, passing below a water trough before turning E. Much later, the path reaches a...

3.15 Road, 1017m. Take the track opposite, SW, and shortly cross another. Then take a right turn to avoid a field. Follow the track around to the SSE, and take a path off left, SE. A few minutes later turn left to the top of the grassy ridge, or pass the grassy hummocks on the right.

View SSW before reaching Cayolar de Mendikotziague

Continue SE, contouring to the right of the next hill ahead, avoiding the path to it. *Another track can be seen below.* Several minutes later the path arrives at some trees and turns SE again, onto the ridge, then to the left, and then back again. Several minutes later the path crosses another and bears right, SE, at a fork. In about 10mins the path turns NE to a farm, continuing NE at a right fork. Fifteen minutes later, fork right, E, and again right, SE, joining a steeply descending track, SE, for about 20mins. Continue on a path SSE, passing a building and gate. A few minutes later, cross a road, to a path, ESE, then cross a stile and down to a road. Turn left, E, and follow down to…

5.40 Logibar, 375m. *This consists of a wayside hotel/restaurant, the Auberge Logibar, with attached gîte on the right. The bar/restaurant is open all day from 15 July to 15 September. Outside this period, it is closed on Wednesdays until 6–7pm, though the gîte remains open. It is popular during the summer as the walk to the Gorges d'Holzarté starts here.*

Day 9: Logibar to Ste-Engrâce

Distance:	23km (14.3 miles)
Height gain:	1187m
Height loss:	932m
Time:	6hrs 50mins
Maps:	IGN Carte de Randonnées No. 2

0.00 Logibar, 375m. Take the access road on the W side of the gîte, cross the bridge and climb the steep path through zigzags. In about 30mins the trail turns sharp left, E, at a sign and climbs steeply. Continue, ignoring turns right then left; the path becomes a track going NE. It passes a stream, then a stile, to join another track. Turn right and follow this more-or-less level track for about 2km. Opposite Pt 999, on the pass, known as...

2.00 Plateau d'Ardakhotchia, 980m. *The Holzarté variant joins from the other direction.* Turn left here, by the sign, and climb the path, SE, that is nearest to the trees. About 20mins later, follow the path, still SE, to the skyline rocks. Shortly after, cross a track, and in another 10mins turn NE to a farm, joining with a track at...

2.35 Abarrakia, 1200m. Turn right and follow this track ESE, and soon S for nearly 1 hour. On a right-hand bend, turn E, and climb a steep path that leads to...

3.50 Col d'Anhaou, 1383m. Turn left onto the track and follow it down to the farm of the same name, Cayolar d'Anhaou. Just before the farm, go down the short cut, NE, to join the track below. Turn left and follow the zigzags down past a water point. Nearly 30mins later, at the next set of zigzags, take a path, ESE, at the first bend. This crosses the track three times to locate an ancient, sunken path to the N, cleared of undergrowth in 2001. This goes down to and passes between two

The GR climbs to the high ground between the Holzarté and Kakouéta gorges and then follows the west side of the latter, though you would mostly be unaware of this. To avoid this, there are two variants. One climbs along the side of Gorge d'Holzarté, and crosses the suspension bridge before turning north to join the current GR10. A check must be made at the auberge that the bridge is still usable. This route takes about an extra hour and cannot be used in the hunting season. The other goes round the east side of the Ravin de Kakouéta, thus avoiding the long road climb at the end of the day. The main route is described here.

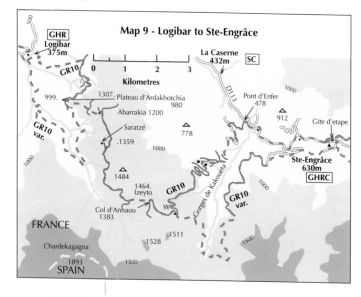

Map 9 - Logibar to Ste-Engrâce

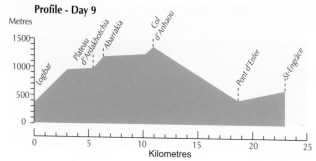

Profile - Day 9

buildings, Granges Errékaltia, then bears left to cross a stream on the right, joining a track on the other side that is followed E. Then take the path ahead, ESE. This soon joins with a track that is followed to a junction. Take the path with a hurdle gateway, ENE. This turns N, crosses a track, and then at a fence line turns NNE. A stream is crossed and shortly a road is followed through bends to the N. About 10mins later, take the track on the right, E, that leads down to the road at...

6.00 Pont d'Enfer, 478m. Climb the very steep short road on the other side to reach the D113. *There is supposed to be a shop at La Caserne, 2km NNW. I did not locate it on a return visit, though it may be in the campsite below the hamlet. If it is very hot, an extra 4km plus all the climbing may not be very inviting. Better to scrounge some food at the auberge.* Turn right on the D113 and climb the road to the gîte at...

6.55 Ste-Engrâce, 630m. *Ste-Engrâce is actually the name of the community that comprises several villages. Auberge Elichalt, opposite the church, runs the gîte, and meals at the auberge are to be savoured.*

Day 10: Ste-Engrâce to Arette-la Pierre-St-Martin

Distance:	12.3km (7.6 miles)
Height gain:	1185m
Height loss:	165m
Time:	4hrs 30mins
Maps:	IGN Carte de Randonnées No. 2

This is an exciting day as we move into really high territory. The karst country ahead contains the first of the high peaks of the Pyrenees. Spectacular contorted limestone scenery provides a dramatic change from the verdant pastures to the west. Superb in fine weather: alas, the last time that I passed through, thick cloud reduced visibility to just a few metres. It would be easy to become disorientated above the Cabane d'Escuret de Bas as the route climbs the grassy convex western slopes of Soum de Leche (1839m); follow the directions carefully.

0.00 Ste-Engrâce, 630m. Go E along the road, and just after the bridge take the lane on the right. Just before another small bridge, turn left along a track, SE, turning E. This crosses a small bridge and another track. Just before a building, take the path SE. This leads into a damp ravine, the ravin d'Arpidia. *This forms the boundary, not only of the local communities of Set-Engrâce and Arette, but also of the Basque provinces of*

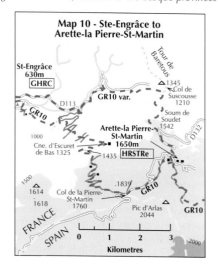

Map 10 - Ste-Engrâce to Arette-la Pierre-St-Martin

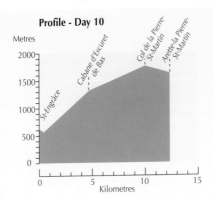

Soule and Béarn. Negotiating the floor of the gully, the trail takes turns right, SW, and then back SE, before climbing out steeply on the left, NNE, about half an hour along the path. This leads to a junction of wide tracks. Turn right along the right branch for a few metres before taking the path off right, S. This climbs steeply through the forest, crossing many forest tracks (too numerous to draw on the sketch map, though described here). After a few minutes, turn left and follow a path going NE, which then turns S. At the next track, continue on the path, E, starting slightly to the left, and immediately take a branch to the SSE. Go straight across the next track, SSW, soon turning right, climbing SSE. At the next track, turn right for a few metres to find the path on the left going back NE. Soon go straight across one and then another track, continuing E. A few minutes later you pass a stile and come to a curious water trough, with the guardian's head carved into the rock. Continue E, to the ruined cabane of…

2.20 Cabane d'Escuret de Bas, 1325m. *It is here that navigation could become difficult in cloud.* Take the path, SW, from the ruin. Maintain this direction, following occasional post markers leading to a clear path around the N and W flanks of Pt 1435 on the map that appears as a grassy hill. Contour the hill to its S side where a post marker and water trough will be seen. From the water trough, across the hollow to the ESE, are some rocks. A clear path and marks again can be found here. Climb the path, ESE, to a second water trough. The area is much furrowed by cattle. Climb above the trough and follow marks, S, and then SW, for a few minutes to yet another water trough and a clear vehicle track. Turn right, S, and follow as it zigzags up the hillside. This leads all the way to the pass, though a short cut can be used across a sharp bend at an obvious hollow, to reach…

3.55 Col de la Pierre-St-Martin, 1760m. *Border with Spain.* Go NE down the road and at the first sharp bend left, take the track on the right, ENE. This becomes a path going N, and then a track again among ski paraphernalia. Climb the right fork, NNE, and a few minutes later take the path to the right, SSE, that leads to the short slope above the…

4.30 Refuge Jeandel, Arette-la Pierre-St-Martin, 1650m. *Jean Hourticq will welcome you at the refuge. The only other place likely to be open is a bar in the ski complex. The shop opens only during July and August and in the ski season. A telephone can be found below the hut beside some garages. I understand that work is underway to provide a small camping area in front of the refuge with cooking, showers and toilet facilities. Some provisions can also be purchased at the refuge.*

Refuge Jeandel, Arette-la Pierre-St-Martin

Day 11: Arette-la Pierre-St-Martin to Lescun

Distance:	15.1km (9.4 miles)
Height gain:	340m
Height loss:	1090m
Time:	5hrs
Maps:	IGN Carte de Randonnées Nos. 2 & 3

0.00 **Arette-la Pierre-St-Martin, 1650m.** Take the track below the refuge that climbs S. Avoid a turning right and three on the left before arriving at a flat area and the Cabane Pastoral de Pescamou. *The HRP bears off to the right while the GR leads left.* Turn left across grass with vehicle tracks, ESE. After a few minutes the path crosses a track and much later, joins a track, E. Soon the trail becomes a wide gravel area. *This can be confusing in cloud, as the tracks are probably ski pistes during the winter. There are ski-lift pylons here also.* Just after a turning to the left, that is ignored, go down, NE, for a

Crossing the lime-stone plateau in poor visibility is not recommended, though I found the waymarking excel-lent, except in one place, and only went off track when I failed to notice change-of-direction marks. The scenery is superb – when you can see it! Below Refuge de Labérouat, the trail is quite complex and unpleasant in wet conditions, espe-cially in the last section, so that the road down to Lescun is inviting for part, if not the whole, way.

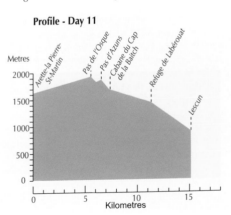

Profile - Day 11

63

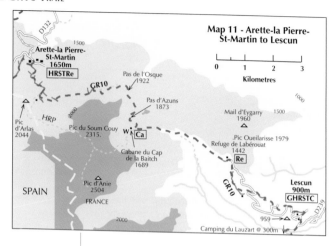

Map 11 - Arette-la Pierre-St-Martin to Lescun

few minutes and take a path to the right. Keep an eye out for a change-of-direction mark which occurs a few minutes later, indicating a right turn. Turn right, SSE, and in about 20mins another change-of-direction-to-the-right mark appears. Turn right, E, following the trail that leads to the bottom of a rocky crest. An easy scramble on the right leads to...

2.10 Pas de l'Osque, 1922m. Cross the bowl to the SE and then S, to reach the enchanting...

2.30 Pas d'Azuns, 1873m. *A place to savour, with Pic d'Anie dominating the scene.* Ascend the ramp with the rock wall on the left until a path drops from the right edge. Follow this down to...

2.45 Cabane du Cap de la Baitch, 1689m. *Water point. This is occupied in the summer and cheese may be for sale, but in the springtime it can be available for walkers.* Follow the path E, which stays high above the valley floor as it enters the woods, with marking infrequent. This can be disconcerting as one is expecting a descent to a village. However, continue, avoiding a path descending to the right, ascending a little from time to time. The path becomes a track a few minutes before arriving at the large building of...

3.55 Refuge de Labérouat, 1442m. *It might be possible to stay here, though it is mainly used for summer holidays. If it is wet, it might be a good idea just to follow the road to Lescun, as the first section of the GR is very muddy and the lower part very wet. The GR is described below.* Go down the road for a few minutes and locate a path going right, SSE. Soon ignore a track to the left, then a path left. The path becomes a muddy farm track heading to the S. Twenty minutes after leaving the road, keep a lookout left for faint traces of a path. Do not continue down to the farm on the clear track. Turn left, NE, and at a junction ignore a path left and another on the right, but take the path by a fence that leads to a track. Turn right, SE, and follow to the road. Cross the road and take the track SE, which after a while becomes a path and crosses another road. Follow the path through fields to where it appears to end in a ditch. Climb the grassy bank to the left, continuing beside the overgrown ditch to a road. Turn left and follow the road round to where a track to the left is indicated. Follow this to another road. Turn right to the centre of...

5.05 Lescun, 900m. *A pretty village in striking scenery. Hotel/restaurant, two gîtes (one run by the hotel), a post office and a shop attached to the hotel provide adequate facilities. There is a camping site just over 1km to the SW of the village on the other side of the valley. A late spring will delay the opening of both the campsite and its shop.*

View from Lescun gîte

65

Day 12: Lescun to Etsaut

The route climbs the valley side to the south-east to the hanging valley at Llers, where the actual route diverges from that shown in the French guide, and then climbs over the next ridge to the Aspe valley, le Gave d'Aspe.

Distance:	16.3km (10.1 miles)
Height gain:	789m
Height loss:	1092m
Time:	5hrs 15mins
Maps:	IGN Carte de Randonnées No. 3

0.00 Lescun, 900m. Go S down the street by the war memorial to the lower road that goes SW to the Pont Moulin (812m). Cross the bridge and directly ahead is a steep track. *This used to be the route but now waymarks follow the road. The old way is still usable and much quicker.* Both ways arrive at the entrance of the campsite. Continue along the road as it winds S. Go straight over a crossroads, and at an island in the road, where a track goes off left, turn left and soon take the path on the right, E. This crosses the road a little

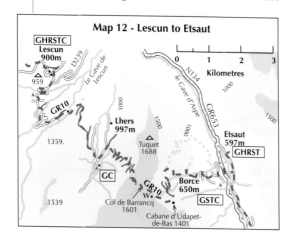

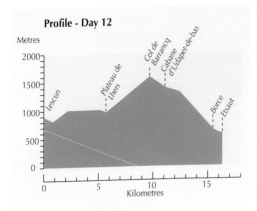

Profile - Day 12

later and continues S. At the road again, turn right for a few metres to locate the path continuing E. Join the road again and follow ENE until this becomes a track. Then take the left fork, NE, and then a path on the right, NE. Go SSE, to the right of the farm ahead, following the path across a small bridge, turning NE into a wood. In about 10mins the path turns round the ridge. Ignore a path on the left and take the left-hand track S. Follow this track, ignoring turnings first left, then right, all the way to a road. Follow SSE to a junction, where there is a gîte on the right and possibility of camping at...

1.40 Plateau de Lhers, 997m. *Booking in advance is necessary, as the owner is not in residence.* Turn left, NNE, at the junction and walk up past a few buildings. Just past one building, take the obvious track right, NE, and then the path on the right, going SSE past a waymarked boulder. After a steep climb across the hillside the path reaches a track. *Another complex climb follows.* Turn right, SSW, and in about 15mins turn left off the main track, taking the right-hand one of two other tracks going E. This soon becomes a path that crosses the track again about 15mins later. After a few minutes more, it joins a track that is followed to the left, round a bend, ignoring another track on the left. It

Lescun

turns SE and then S. Then, at another bend, ignore the track on the right, but soon after take the path on the right that turns towards the E. Only a few minutes later turn left onto another track, for a few metres, to find the path that goes off right, SSE. Shortly, join a track, continuing SSE to a path on the left, that in a few minutes reaches...

3.20 Col de Barrancq, 1601m. *If the weather is fine, 200m to the SW is a wonderful view over the Aspe valley. There is a water source at the ruined hut below.* Follow the path down, E, passing the ruined cabane (1515m) and on to the lower one...

3.45 Cabane d'Udapet-de-Bas, 1401m. The trail passes just below the cabane to a track going NW. In a few minutes, take the path, N. Twenty minutes or so later, take the path, SE, that zigzags down through the bracken, crosses a stream and goes down to a road. Turn left, N, and follow the bends for a few minutes before taking the path off left, ENE, that goes down to another road. Do not cross the bridge ahead but turn right and follow the road across a junction, SE, which soon leads into...

5.00 Borce, 650m. *The gîte and shop are beside the church. The campsite and another smaller gîte are above the village to the S.* Walk N, through the village, but before going down the steep access road too far, take a grassy path right, E, that goes down to a small footbridge over a stream and reaches the N134. Cross the road; if it is busy, use the footbridge to the left, and go across the bridge opposite, passing the remains of the old railway track. Turn left at the junction and go N into...

5.15 Etsaut, 597m. *Hotel/restaurant, shop, and the gîte with only breakfast available, is in the compound of the Maison des Jeunes et de la Culture, situated to the E of the main square. There is another gîte, opposite the hotel, that doesn't look very inviting. The SNCF bus service from Oloron-Ste-Marie to Canfranc, in Spain, via the Col du Somport, passes through here.*

Day 13: Etsaut to Gabas

Distance:	24.7km (15.4 miles)
Height gain:	1588m
Height loss:	1158m
Time:	7hrs 20mins
Maps:	IGN Carte de Randonnées No. 3

The GR takes to the Chemin de la Mâture today. The year 1772 saw the completion of a sloping way cut into the rock face to bring suitable trees down through the Sescoué ravine for the French Navy. Today, part is still usable and the GR10 takes advantage of it. It is quite spectacular, easy to climb and only those who suffer from extreme vertigo would have problems. A super section is walked today, with the classic view of Pic du Midi d'Ossau, reflected in Lac Gentau. The route doesn't follow the French guide route from Etsaut since the new bypass was opened.

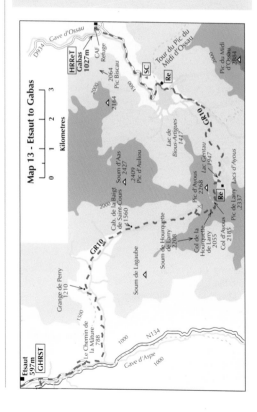

Chemin de la Mâture

0.00 Etsaut, 597m. Follow the road, S, from Etsaut, passing the bridge crossed upon arrival and on to another bridge, Pont de Cebers, that gives access to the N134. Don't cross the bridge but continue up the sign-posted lane ahead until, at a sharp bend left, take the path that at first goes SW. This is the start of...

0.35 Chemin de la Mâture, 788m. As the trail turns to the E, the Fort du Portalet comes into view and the section cut into the rock begins. The trail turns towards the N, leaving the Chemin (which crossed the ravine

Snow isn't normally a problem by the second half of June. It would be a good idea, though, to ask about the snow condition on the passes before leaving Etsaut.

71

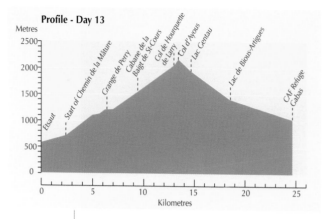

Profile - Day 13

by a bridge, now missing). At the top of a very steep section, take the right fork E and follow to pass to the right of...

1.25 Grange de Perry, 1210m. About 15mins later, turn left, N, and some 7–10mins further, take the right fork to cross a bridge and follow the path, SE. After another bridge, fork right, SE and continue to...

3.00 Cabane de la Baigt de St-Cours, 1560m. *Shepherds may be in residence during the summer. The Parc National des Pyrénées starts here.* Continue S, along the path, crossing to the left bank. At the start of the steep section turn NW to climb the long zigzags to the rocky pass of...

4.30 Col de Hourquette de Larry, 2055m. *The HRP joins here.* A couple of minutes later, turn right, S, and continue to...

4.40 Col d'Ayous, 2185m. Take the obvious path, E, steeply down towards the lakes, bearing right to...

5.00 Refuge d'Ayous, 1960m. *Popular refuge providing accommodation and meals. The comparatively isolated walking is transformed by crowds enjoying the spectacular scenery, weather permitting.* Pick up the GR a few minutes to the E, below, and follow to a track leading to...

6.20 Lac de Bious-Artigues, 1417m. *Refuge Pyrénéa Sports provides accommodation and meals and there are two of cafés adjacent. The trail passes Camping de Bious-Oumette, complete with shop, 1km below. Follow the road down to a short cut, just before the main road. To go to the village, turn left down the path, NNE, to the road and turn down left. To go to the refuge, continue to the main road and turn left also. The refuge is just on the opposite side of the road at…*
7.20 Gabas, 1027m. *Hotels, telephone, but no shop in the village. Accommodation and meals are available at the refuge above the village, where a welcome awaits.*

Pic du Midi d'Ossau

Day 14: Gabas to Gourette

Distance:	22.5km (14 miles)
Height gain:	1468m
Height loss:	1149m
Time:	8hrs 25mins
Maps:	IGN Carte de Randonnées No. 3

The Hourquette d'Arre can hold snow well into the summer. Ascertain its condition before departure! Typically, the final ascent to the pass (though steep) can be climbed without special snow equipment. However, beyond there is 1km of high, north-facing plateau, with 400m of steep, north-facing gullies that descend to Lac d'Anglas. This area can remain snow-covered even longer. There's another narrow cliff traverse today, with a cable giving some protection, but it doesn't have the sense of exposure as that experienced on Day 13, probably because the crag below is tree-covered.

0.00 Gabas, 1027m. Take the track beside the refuge that joins the D934 higher up. Follow the road, E, for 10mins or so, and then turn left over a bridge. A signpost indicates the way. The path goes WNW to pass above Gabas, taking a sharp turn right, E, before continuing N. The path becomes a track that joins another. Turn left, NW, and about 15mins later, after a short descent, take the path right, ENE, and almost straightaway, take a right fork, ESE, to…

1.30 La Corniche des Alhas, 1130m. *It is possible to avoid this by descending the forest track to the Pont du Goua (966m), then climbing back up again on the other side.* Negotiate the ledge, taking extra care while crossing an avalanche chute, to arrive at a bridge. Cross the bridge and follow the path NW, then N to the junction with the alternative route. Soon the path turns NE, passes the path on the right coming from the Soussouéou valley, and starts a long and very steep climb. Eventually, easier ground is reached above the trees. About 15mins later there is a turning left, NW, that goes to the Cabanes de Cézy. *The local herdsmen allow camping at the huts, and there is water available at the huts. I understand that there is a small, low hut, nearer to the GR, behind the hummock on the right, that can also be used. Le petit train de l'Artouste may be seen contouring the mountainside on the far side of the valley, just below 2000m.* The GR turns right, E, and climbs easily until, much later, it climbs more

Soussouéou valley. The little yellow train crosses above the trees to the right

steeply. After an even steeper section it passes a water point and within a few minutes arrives at the…

4.30 Stream crossing, 1860m. Cross the stream and follow the narrow path, to the NE, above the stream. About 20mins later, the trail turns S, passes a small tarn and goes SE across a bowl to a junction beyond the high ground at

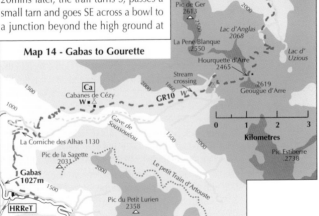

Map 14 - Gabas to Gourette

75

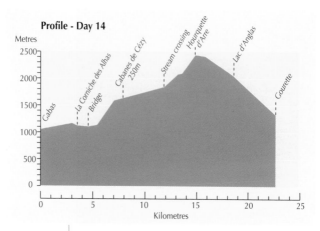

Profile - Day 14

the far end of the bowl. Turn left and climb to…

6.30 Hourquette d'Arre, 2465m. *The fairly easy descent to the lake below to the E, unfortunately, is not the target! Small shelter to the E of pass.* Follow waymarks N, from the pass. If they are covered in snow, footprints should lead the way. After the initial descent, the trail goes NE, then N, and then NW, before starting the steep descent, NE to…

7.25 Lac d'Anglas, 2068m. Follow the trail, N, from the lake, and after 25–30mins it joins a track. Turn right and follow the track N, ignoring another path coming from the right. Pass the Cabanes de Coste de Goua, seen to the right, and within a few minutes another track is joined that comes from the right and immediately take the path off right, N. *The striking Arête du Sarrière is seen to the left.* About 15mins later, the path goes straight across another track before arriving at a junction just before the Pont de Saxe, with the tennis courts beyond. One can either cross the bridge and climb to the road above the tennis courts and turn down left, or turn left at the junction and climb to a chalet and then down a track to…

8.25 Gourette, 1346m. *Gourette is a large ski town spread out over the slopes above a bend in the D918*

road that climbs to the Col d'Aubisque. A crag above the town gives it a spectacular setting. The CAF refuge is situated at the far N of the town, behind the last hotel, slightly uphill from the large car-park apron. Some provisions can be bought at the refuge. This is the only place that is likely to be open outside of July and August and the ski season, with the exception of a couple of bars. I understand that the Club Pyrénéa refuge, just before the CAF one, should also be open, though it seemed closed when I was there in June 2001. There is also a campsite or wild camp area just over 1km N, down the D918. It is possible to accompany the guardian down to Laruns if he is going there to obtain supplies.

Sharp ridge above Gourette

Day 15: Gourette to Arrens-Marsous

A much easier day, crossing two lower passes. The first leads to the D918 between the Aubisque and Soulor passes of Tour de France fame. The other allows a direct route to Arrens-Marsous and to the D918 once more.

Distance:	14km (8.7 miles)
Height gain:	640m
Height loss:	1108m
Time:	4hrs 30mins
Maps:	IGN Carte de Randonnées No.3

0.00 Gourette, 1346m. From the refuge go back to the road with the bars and at the end, at the noticeboard, bear left and follow the track under the telecabina cables SE to a small chalet. Just before the chalet, take the path left and follow down to and across the bridge below. Climb past the tennis courts to the road and turn right. Soon, at a signpost, take the track right, E, that climbs in zigzags above Gourette. Take a path on the right that climbs away from Gourette to...

1.30 Col de Tortes, 1799m. Go down the path, NE, taking a right fork later, also NE. This goes down to the road just as it turns to the E, the...

2.00 D918, 1400m. *In summer, sheep's cheese can be*

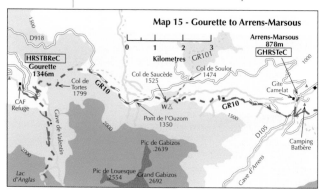

78

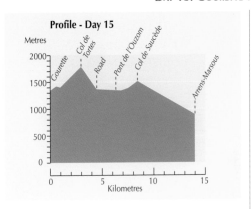

Profile - Day 15

purchased 250m to the left. It is possible to avoid the road in bad snow conditions by following the trail down into the valley and climbing back out again. This should only be necessary in the very early part of the season and should not affect coast-to-coast walkers. Follow the road E, passing to the left of a road tunnel and then through a second. Two inviting streams are passed, but remember that there are grazing grounds in the hanging valleys above! Pont de l'Ouzom crosses the second stream, and just as the road begins to climb to the Col de Soulor, turn right, ESE, onto a path that climbs to...

3.00 Col de Saucède, 1525m. *There is a water pipe here. The access GR101 from Lourdes joins from the track on the left.* A short distance left along the track, take the path, ENE, and then right at a fork that passes to the right of a building. Cross the stream and follow the path to a grassy ridge where post markers lead the way. Turn off the ridge to the NE and then back right to another stream. Follow the stream left before crossing it a little lower down to reach a farm and track. Follow the track, ENE, to a road where you turn right, E, for a few metres. Take the path right, E, to join the road again, continuing E. At a left bend, take the track, ESE, which in a few minutes reaches another road, the D105. Turn left and follow into...

Col de Tortes

4.30 Arrens-Marsous, 878m. *There is a gîte signposted to the right on the way in, but most people try to book into the one in town – the Gîte Auberge Camelat – as the meals are renowned. Booking in advance is certainly recommended. The nearest campsite is Camping Batbère (see the sketch map for location). There is a supermarket just NE of town, a hotel, post office, tourist office and pharmacy.*

Day 16: Arrens-Marsous to Cauterets

Distance:	27.1km (16.8 miles)
Height gain:	1574m
Height loss:	1539m
Time:	9hrs 15mins
Maps:	IGN Carte de Randonnées No. 3

0.00 Arrens-Marsous, 878m. Follow the road S from the town and take the left fork at the junction, instead of following the D105. Cross the Gave d'Azun by an old bridge, taking the track, E. At the junction, take the centre one of the three tracks, NE. This soon becomes a path. Follow this E, and ignoring paths joining from the right, at a fork, take the right-hand path E. In a few minutes, take the left fork and then immediately turn back right, NE. This meets the road, which is followed to the left, NE. In a few minutes, at a bend, go E on a path to the road again, and turn left, E. This leads to...

This is a long day, in two parts, with lots of climbing and descending. After the first pass, the route goes down to the Gave de Labat. The GR uses the road as well as taking to paths and tracks on either side from time to time, though the road can be followed all the way to Lac d'Estaing. After that the GR finds an easy way over a fine ridge that looks intimidating on approach.

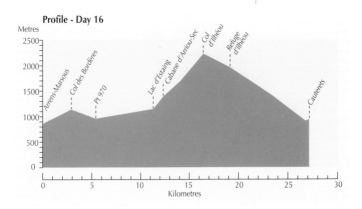

Profile - Day 16

1.10 Col des Bordéres, 1156m. *The GR takes short cuts across the road, though the road could be followed.* Just after the sign, take the path left, between two buildings. This soon meets the road again, which is followed S. At a junction, take a path on the right, SE, back to the road, going right. Soon take another path SE that turns left, NE, before crossing the road and joining it yet again. Turn left, NE, and then right, SE, to the church. Cross grass around the church to find a path going SW. This goes down to a road, the D103 and crosses it to a bridge, Pt 970. *The D103 can be followed all the way to the lake, which is especially useful if it is wet.* There are several campsites beside the road, a bar/restaurant and a gîte, all marked on the sketch map. On the other side of the bridge, turn right, S, along a road, and soon right at a fork, SSW. This becomes a path going S to the road again. Just ahead, cross the road and a bridge, taking a path S, now on

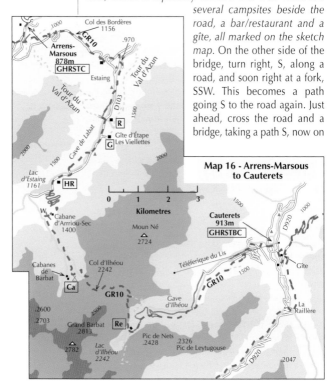

Summer resident near Col d'Ihéou

the W side of the D103. A few minutes later, pass through a gate and in another few minutes, join a track going SSW to another gate. Then at the road, turn right, cross the bridge and continue along the D103, S. About 1.5km later, cross a bridge on the right, taking a path, W, at first, before turning SW to reach a farm. Follow the farm road down to a bridge and back to the D103 for the last time. Follow the road, SW, to the...

3.10 Lac d'Estaing, 1161m. *The Hotel Restaurant du Lac d'Estaing should be open from the beginning of May until mid-October. It is evident from all the facilities in this valley that it is very popular in the holiday season.* Follow the road around the lake for a few minutes, and at a sign turn left up a steep path through the wood, SW. This crosses a track six times in a southerly direction before turning SW, taking the left branch at a junction to reach the...

3.50 Cabane d'Arriou-Sec, 1400m. *I understand that there is a water source nearby.* Follow the path W, across a track, and then a path, S. The trail gently climbs the right of the valley, SE. Much later it crosses a small foot-bridge to a junction below two cabanes, the Cabanes de Barbat, one of stone and the other of metal, painted green. Turn E, and later SE, for the hard climb to…

6.20 Col d'Ilhéou, 2242m. A sign shows the way to the NE, then E, and 20mins later, at a sign, the path turns sharply NW, before continuing S to…

7.05 Refuge d'Ilhéou, 1988m. *Situated just above the lake of the same name. Be warned that this is a very expensive place.* Follow the track down, NE, until a path goes off right at a left bend. Take the path, NE, down to the track and follow it SE, a little way, before turning left, N, onto a path. This is followed, crossing the track again, E. Twenty minutes later the path joins the track once more, E, and then soon turns off right, NE, just before the bridge. Take the left turn at a fork, NE, some time later. After the way becomes vague, bear left at another fork, going down NE, to a fence to the left. The path continues, NE, with the fence on the left. The path becomes a track and joins a road. Turn left, and in 2–3mins take the path on the right, W, that shortly joins a track. Turn right, E, and again, in a couple of minutes,

Lac d'Ilhéou

take the path left, NE. This joins a road; turn left, ignore a turning to the left, and follow the bend to the SE. A few minutes later take the path to the left that goes down E. That turns sharply to the N before going down E to a road on the outskirts of the town. Go straight across the road ahead and down steps, taking one of the roads right into…

9.15 Cauterets, 913m. *This is a real oasis for trekkers and all facilities are available, including bus services to Lourdes with connections to Luz and Gavarnie, and another service to Pont d'Espagne, which might be of interest to those who wish to walk the three-day variant via the Hourquette d'Ossoue (2734m). Please note that this service leaves from the town centre at 8am, with the next at 10am. Re-sealable gas cylinders and mountain equipment are also on sale. The pleasant gîte can be found at 25 Rue du Maréchal Joffre, a short climb to the SE of town. There is another, on the Rue de la Raillère to the S.*

Day 17: Cauterets to Luz-St-Sauveur

Another heavy day, but many zigzags mean that the gradients are easy.

Distance:	22km (13.7 miles)
Height gain:	1248m
Height loss:	1441m
Time:	7hrs
Maps:	IGN Carte de Randonnées No. 4

0.00 Cauterets, 913m. The GR leaves between the two thermal baths, Le Rocher and César, on the E of town. Go up the steps and follow the path, behind the latter, as it zigzags to a road above. *If you are staying at the gîte Beau Soleil, it is better to continue up the road, SSE, and at the bend, turn left at a large crucifix. Follow the road to meet the other path, seen as steps on the left. The variant turns right from here.* Turn left along the road to a bridge, where it becomes a track. There are few waymarks, but follow the track through zigzags upward.

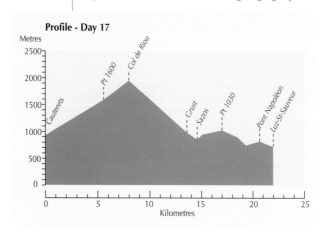

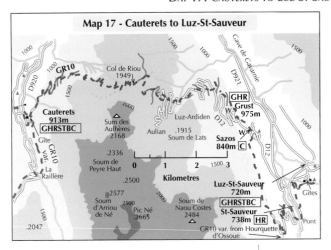

Map 17 - Cauterets to Luz-St-Sauveur

About 75mins from the steps, just after a right bend, take the path on the left that turns back NE, and passes through an iron gate. This crosses a track with the path on the other side starting a little to the left, going ESE. Follow this path ever upwards, and about 1 hour later, at a junction, turn sharp left, NE, to more zigzags and finally...

3.00 Col de Riou, 1949m. Take the track, NE, and some minutes later turn off the track onto a path that goes down to another path. Turn right, SW, and about 15mins later turn N under a ski lift and onto a wide grassy track, NE. Ignore a track right, and just before the track turns right and passes below, short cut the bend by a path on the right. Follow the track down a short way before taking a path, S, at the next bend. This comes to a large parking area. Cross this and join the road going down N. The GR cuts across bends in the road. Firstly, take a path on the right, S, down to the road, and turn right, SE. Two minutes later go left on a path, N, down to the road again and turn left, N. After another 2mins turn back, on the right, down the path and straight across the next road section to the NE and then E, along the edge of a field. At the next road, bear right to the path, SSE. Go left, NNE, at the road again taking a track to the right, NE, and then a path going off to the left, NE. Several minutes later, cross the road, E, cross a track, N. The path then turns to the E. Cross the road yet again, E, then a track, ESE. At the next road section turn right, SSE, to locate the path going off N, and the cross a track, SE, and then another, continuing in the same direction, SE. In about 10–15mins arrive in…

4.55 Grust, 975m. *You can treat yourself to an expensive beer at the auberge! There is a hotel/restaurant and gîte here. Water next to the track.* At the bottom of the village, take the path on the left, S, which joins the road in a few minutes, the D12. Here you turn left, N, to go round the bend to another path that goes off N, then turns to the SE, to...

5.10 Sazos, 840m. *At the bottom of the village there is a campsite. From here it is about 40mins down the road to the gîtes at Luz, but it will probably take longer if it is hot. The GR takes the high, contouring route, before going down to Pont Napoléon, which takes over twice as long. It is a very pleasant walk after the initial steep section to the farm above and across the D12. The main advantage of the longer route is that it is shaded for nearly all the way, whereas the road is extremely hot in afternoon sunshine.* Through Sazos, it is important to keep to the higher narrow road until a turn right, by a water trough, up a narrow, steep lane can be taken. Soon a steep path goes up right, SSW, to the D12, where the steep road on the other side is climbed. Turn right at the top and go up the path, W, which turns left to the farm. A right, WSW, then left through the farm buildings, locates the path on the other side going S. Nearly 40mins later, ignore a path going down left, and in a few more minutes the path comes out onto a road by a cross. *The road can be followed all the way down to Pont Napoléon.* For the GR10, follow the road down, S, past a turning on the right and then a short cut on the left, hardly seen and not really needed. Another on the right is much clearer. On the road again a clear track is taken to the left, W, and not so obviously, but almost immediately, above, on the bank at the right, a path right is taken. This comes down to the road again that is followed down past a right-hand bend and then a track is taken on the left, N. Shortly, take the path on the right, E, that zigzags down to the road, the D921. Turn right and in a few minutes arrive at...

6.30 Pont Napoléon, 755m. Cross the bridge and turn left for 400m. Just after a private driveway on the right, take the wide path, also on the right, signposted Solfério. Follow this to the church, cross the grassy mound on the right, or just follow the trail around to a track going E, down from the church to a small bridge on the left. Cross the bridge to the first campsite, on the right with gîte, and with another gîte on the left at...

7.00 Luz-St-Sauveur, 720m. *The main part of the town is 500m to the N, past the fortified church. There is another campsite with its entrance on the E of the main square. Luz also has the usual services.*

Hospitaller church, Luz-St-Sauveur

Day 18: Luz-St-Sauveur to Barèges

A fairly easy day after an initially steep ascent. An alternative local route starts at the castle of Sainte-Marie, passing through the villages of Esterre, Viella, Viey and Sers. I have rarely seen vipers during over 4000km of walking in the Pyrenees, but on my last trip I nearly tripped over two, on either side of the River Bolou. Beware!

Distance:	12.1km (7.5 miles)
Height gain:	832m
Height loss:	312m
Time:	3hrs 50mins
Maps:	IGN Carte de Randonnées No. 4

0.00 Luz-St-Sauveur, 720m. Go back over the bridge by the campsite and gîtes, turn left and follow the path to a road. Follow this around a sharp left bend, over a bridge, and take the path right, E, and then left, after the building. Ten minutes later, turn right onto a track to locate the path turning off left a few metres further on. Climb steeply past a level path on the left, continuing SE, to cross an irrigation canal. Continue E, to where the path turns onto the ridge beside a stone wall, at the…

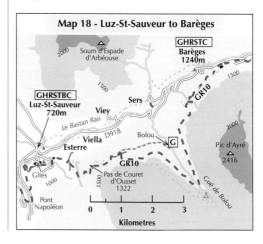

Map 18 - Luz-St-Sauveur to Barèges

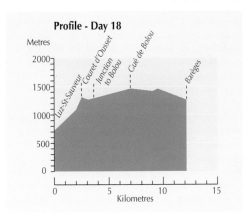

1.15 Couret d'Ousset, 1322m. Go down through the wood to a signpost and junction. Ignore the path joining from the left, and the one turning left, and go straight on, NE. The path soon becomes a track and a few minutes later, at a gate, the track forks. *The left-hand branch goes to the gîte at Bolou.* Take the right branch, NE, and a few minutes later turn right onto a path going S. There are not many waymarks for a while, but follow the path as it turns ENE, passes below a water trough, and continues clearly and fairly level into the Bolou valley. Follow the path SE, and just after a signpost, cross the…

2.30 Gué de Bolou, 1460m. Cross the stream and follow the obvious and fairly level path NNW. Eventually turn left, NW, down towards farm buildings, and then right, NE, a few minutes later. In another 4–5mins, ignore a path on the right but go down ESE to cross a wooded gully, to continue on the path seen below and on the left. Near to Barèges, take a left fork, NNE, to arrive beside the gîte l'Hospitalet at…

3.50 Barèges, 1240m. *There is another gîte below and to the right of the first one, which is called Oasis. The town is spread out along the D918, with most of the facilities W of the GR10 point of arrival. The campsite*

Luz-St-Sauveur is nearly 1km away, at the bottom of the village, after the first zigzag. However, the road can be avoided by taking a route beside the river that starts at the fire station. An English couple run the hotel, Les Sorbiers, but no evening meal is served on Wednesdays.

Day 19: Barèges to Chalet-Hôtel de l'Oule

Distance:	22.7km (14.1 miles)
Height gain:	1309m
Height loss:	728m
Time:	7hrs 50mins
Maps:	IGN Carte de Randonnées No. 4

If it is at all possible, do wait for good weather before tackling this part of the route as the scenery is to be savoured. Camping is only allowed below the earth dam of Lac d'Aubert as the many signs indicate. It is possible to shorten the day by using the chalet-hôtel at Lac d'Orédon, following the trail past Lac d'Aubert. The usual snow warnings apply for the high pass, though by late June there shouldn't be any problem.

0.00 Barèges, 1240m. From the gîte l'Hospitalet go down the narrow lane, NE, past the other gîte and take a path off right, ENE. After a few minutes this joins a road, which is followed E past a turn to the left. Within a minute, take the track right, E, that soon ends. Take the path right that becomes a track again, going down to the main road, D918. Turn right and 10mins later, at a fork, take the road left, E, and pass the Auberge Couquelle to a large car-parking area. From here, go along the track SE that soon joins one coming from the left. Follow this right, S, until a path to the left is indicated, NE at first and then SSE, avoiding a turning to the left. This is followed, S, to the D918 again, just above the...

1.10 Pont de la Gaubie. 1538m. Cross the road and follow the path to a track, which is followed S. At the end of the track, at a signpost, take the path left, E. Ascend the lovely valley and after 30mins cross the stream, firstly to the S and then back N, in an area suitable for camping. Continue to the ESE, and in 40mins or so take the right branch of the path to...

3.20 Cabane d'Aygues-Cluses, 2150m. *Suitable for emergency use. The climb to the col is not difficult.* Follow the trail, just W of S, to the Lacs de Madamète, continuing around boulders to reach...

4.40 Col de Madamète, 2509m. *Superb views! This is highest pass on the GR10, only surpassed by the Hourquette d'Ossoue on the three-day option, passing*

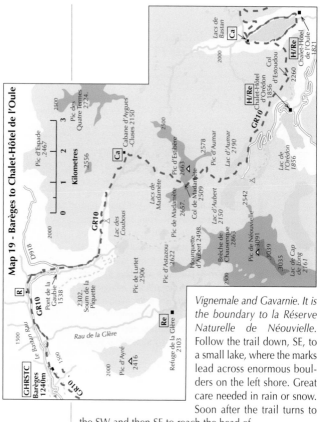

Map 19 - Barèges to Chalet-Hôtel de l'Oule

Vignemale and Gavarnie. It is the boundary to la Réserve Naturelle de Néouvielle. Follow the trail down, SE, to a small lake, where the marks lead across enormous boulders on the left shore. Great care needed in rain or snow. Soon after the trail turns to the SW and then SE to reach the head of...

5.30 Lac d'Aumar, 2190m. Follow the path around the W side of the lake to the turning to the camping area and Chalet-Hôtel Orédon (a sign says 'bivouac 15 minutes'). Continue following the lake edge and cross a bridge by the EDF building to a road. Either follow the road ESE, or the path to the left of it, and as the road turns away from the lake, take the path, E, which begins to turn to the SE, climbing through a wood to...

6.50 Col d'Estoudou, 2260m. *The path up from Lac*

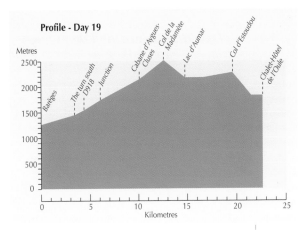

d'Orédon joins from the right. Take the path, ENE, and follow down to Lac d'Oule and a track. *The GR officially turns left but only for those who have stayed at the Orédon refuge or who want to camp at the head of the lake. Follow the trail, left to the head of the lake, cross a bridge and continue E, to Cabane de la Lude.* To reach accommodation beside Lac de l'Oule, turn right and follow the track southwards to the dam. Cross the dam to...

7.50 Chalet-Hôtel de l'Oule, 1821m. *A busy place providing full refuge/mountain hotel services.*

Cabane de la Lude and Lac de l'Oule

Day 20: Chalet-Hôtel de l'Oule to Vielle-Aure

Above the lake, to the east, is an area of ski lifts. The GR avoids most of this by taking a higher route to the N. Then follows a long and easy ridge descent.

Distance:	16.3km (10.1 miles)
Height gain:	394m
Height loss:	1415m
Time:	4hrs 50mins
Maps:	IGN Carte de Randonnées No. 4

0.00 Chalet-Hôtel de l'Oule, 1821m. On the N side of the refuge, go steeply up the track to the right that gains a little height above the lake. Follow the track above, N, to the end of the lake, just above the Cabane de la Lude. *This cabane is usually locked, but I noticed that it had housed a number of youths during a storm.* Turn right and climb steeply to the E, and SE, above the lake. Twenty minutes later, turn sharp left, N, to climb past the Cabane de Bastan. Continue ENE to a…

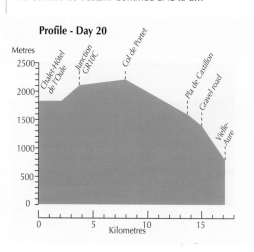

1.10 Junction with the GR10C, 2110m. Turn right, S, and follow the more-or-less level path as it turns to the E. The path crosses two streams and then bears right at a fork, S, before turning to the E again. Within 15mins from the junction the path joins a track coming from the left. Another track comes up from the right. Continue straight ahead at the junction, NE. In 2mins you reach…

2.10 Col de Portet, 2215m. *There was much work being done by bulldozers as I passed, and the path N had been obliterated. At the pass, one track goes up to the large building seen to the SE. Another goes down to the NE, and yet another to the N. Go N, until the path soon appears. In about 5mins, take the right fork, E. The trail follows the right-hand side of the ridge, just above the road, until the road turns down through zigzags to the south. Thirty-five minutes later the path passes through a rocky defile and waymarks appear again. About* another 30mins later, pass through a staggered fence system and soon you come to a grassy saddle with a large post on it and another to the left at…

3.20 Pla de Castillon, 1606m. There is a clear path going to the hill ahead. Do not go along this path but turn right to a fence line. There is a waymark on a boulder by the large post. *I have a suspicion that a faint path going off right, just before the pass, might also go to the fence.* Follow the fence down to a gravel road.

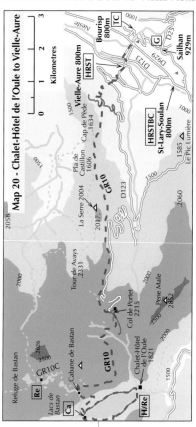

97

Summer snow on the Néouvielle

Turn right down the gravel road and at the first right bend, take the path, N. Thirty minutes later, cross a road and follow the path on the other side that zigzags down to the road again. Turn to the right to locate the path going down, NE, and within a few minutes the road is joined once more and is followed E, to...

4.50 Vielle-Aure, 800m. *This village is on the outskirts and indeed is really part of the sprawling mass of St-Lary-Soulan, with its ski industry higher up. The campsite can be found just along the road to Bourisp. Meals can be had at the bar/restaurant opposite the tourist office. Unfortunately, the gîte is now closed, so ask at the tourist office for the latest accommodation details. Turning right at the tourist office leads to hotel, tabac and épicerie. There is another campsite opposite the supermarket, S on the D929. There is also a gîte at Sailhan to the SE.*

Day 21: Vielle-Aure to Germ

Distance:	13km (8.1 miles)
Height gain:	1165m
Height loss:	626m
Time:	4hrs 30mins
Maps:	IGN Carte de Randonnées No. 5

The GR10 more or less follows the line of D225 road, using footpaths, with a stiff climb to Germ. There are a number of water points in the initial villages.

0.00 Vielle-Aure, 800m. Cross the bridge and immediately turn left and then right along Rue du Moulin. This quiet lane brings you to the main road, D929. Cross the road, pass Camping La Mousquère, and follow the road left over the bridge into the village of Bourisp. After the bridge, ignore the track right but take the next concrete track, E, between buildings, that soon becomes a path leading to a chapel. Pass between the memorial and the chapel to a wide grassy trail and enter the wood. Follow the path to the road, D225, and the hamlet of Estensan (1004m). Ignore the D25 on the right, following the D225 to the water point. Take the narrow road right at the fork. As the surfaced road ends, turn left up a track, S, and

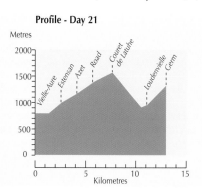

Profile - Day 21

99

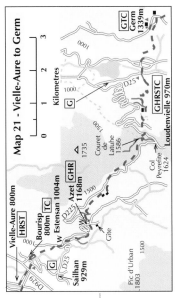

Map 21 - Vielle-Aure to Germ

follow to the road again. Turn right and follow around a left bend to the path off right, ENE, which goes to the road again at…

1.05 Azet, 1168m. Follow the road, again around a left-hand bend, steeply past the church and water point, ignoring a turning off right. Go NE, up the road. Take a steep track right, NE, and turn right again at a junction and shortly turn left, N, up another track. Ignore a track left as the track turns to the SE. This soon becomes a shaded path climbing E. Passing buildings on the right, the Granges de Goutes, the path bears left to the road. Cross the road and take the path that bypasses a gate, SE. The path can soon be seen ahead, climbing all the way to the pass, just above the road, seen on the right. A short steep section leads to…

2.30 Couret de Latuhe, 1586m. *The Col de Peyrefite is about 500m to the S. The route can be confusing here, especially if the hillside is covered with people and their vehicles awaiting a view of the Tour de France.* Turn left at the track and go N, for 100m or so, to locate a small concrete marker with a No.1 cast in it. *This is the key to the descent, but care in navigation is still needed for the initial part.* Turn right onto the path, ESE, turning SE. A few minutes later, cross the road, going NE. Again, a few minutes later, cross the road onto the path, E, that soon turns S across grass to a steep bank. Continue S to another path, where you turn left, E. This brings you, in a few minutes, to a five-way junction and sign to Loudenvielle. Do not follow the signed way but take the path down, beside the stone wall, SE. Follow waymarks E, to a farm, Granges de Paulède, where the path turns right to a track that is followed NE. Soon, take the right fork and in a few minutes, go right, NE, on a path. In about 3mins, turn sharp right off the path to another going

down steeply, S. This comes to a track that is taken NE and then turning to the E. It becomes a path and then a track again down past the campsite to the D25 and across the bridge to…

Couret de Latuhe on Tour de France day

3.30 Loudenvielle, 970m. *Some shops can be seen on the right. These include a mini-supermarket, tabac, tourist office and pharmacy.* Walk up through the village, passing two water points, to the post office, where a sign to Germ points the way, on the left and up a path, ENE. *Though often in shade, this can be a demanding climb in the heat of the day. Take your time!* Very much later, the path joins another; turn sharp left, NE, and again, NE, at another junction a few minutes later by a signpost. At the road, turn left and climb a short distance to the access track to the gîte on the right; just before there is a short cut across the grass, also to the right.

4.30 Germ, 1339m. *Camping is allowed on the grassy terraces and there is a swimming pool. This is a delightful place, with helpful staff even when busy. Other accommodation can be found at an auberge at the E end of the hamlet. The public telephone is between them.*

Day 22: Germ to Lac d'Oô

Distance:	15.7km (9.8 miles)
Height gain:	1176m
Height loss:	1011m
Time:	5hrs 45mins
Maps:	IGN Carte de Randonnées No. 5

A pleasant walk early in the morning, followed by a steep climb to the pass. The last part of the descent to the Granges d'Astau is exceedingly steep, eased by long zigzags and a view back which causes one to wonder whoever found the route originally. It might be tempting, if it is hot, to use the facilities at the gîte and restaurant, rather than continue to Lac d'Oô, but that would leave an awful lot to do the next day. It would be a good idea to book ahead at Chez Tintin (Tel: 05.61.79.12.29).

0.00 Germ, 1339m. Go back through the hamlet and, as the road bears right, take the track left, SSE, ignoring three other tracks that join from the left, until a path is taken to the left, SSW, about 15mins later. The path curves round to the SE, and goes down E through a defile to a landslip. The route is marked to climb above this and I would suggest that it is better to follow this and not cross the hard slope without great care and using a walking stick. The path comes to a small dammed pool and another landslip that can be passed either above or

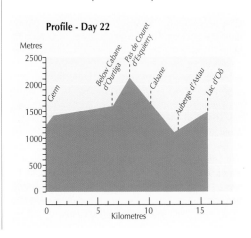

Profile - Day 22

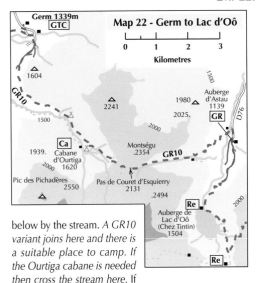

below by the stream. *A GR10 variant joins here and there is a suitable place to camp. If the Ourtiga cabane is needed then cross the stream here. If not*, continue on the right bank to below the…

1.35 Cabane d'Ourtiga, 1600m. *The hut above can be used by walkers.* Cross the stream and follow waymarks steeply upwards, generally SE. About 40mins later a fairly level path is joined; turn right, SW. Thirty minutes later the trail passes through a stony, shallow gully. Ignore a route to the right, marked with red paint, that continues up the gully, but cross the gravel bank on the left, E, to find more waymarks and follow the trail to…

3.00 Pas de Couret d'Esquierry, 2131m. *The border between the Départements Haute Pyrénées and Haute Garonne. Traces of a route to the S indicate a way to the Espingo hut, but it is very difficult and not recommended by the authorities.* Go down the other side of the pass and after about 10mins, take the left fork, E, and then, after another 10mins or so, at another fork, go right, E. A few minutes later, cross a stream (possibility of water) and continue to below a cabin. *There is no need to go to the cabin; but if you do, don't continue on the path leaving from the hut but come back to the stream.* Cross

Auberge d'Astau

the stream, continue E, and soon enter the wood. Follow the zigzags down to the open pasture below and follow the path NE to some buildings to the left of a bridge. Cross the bridge, turn right and climb the road to the gîte and...

4.35 Auberge d'Astau, 1139m. *This is a very popular area, especially at weekends.* Follow the track S, which becomes rougher and boulder-strewn. Follow the mule track to...

5.45 Lac d'Oô, 1504m. *The private refuge/café, Chez Tintin, is across the dam to the right. The spectacular waterfall, at the end of the lake, the Cascade d'Oô, has been famous since Victorian times.*

Day 23: Lac d'Oô to Bagnères-de-Luchon

Distance:	18.5km (11.5 miles)
Height gain:	1003m
Height loss:	1857m
Time:	6hrs 50mins
Maps:	IGN Carte de Randonnées No. 5

0.00 Lac d'Oô, 1504m. Follow the trail round the E of the lake. It starts to climb across the very steep slope below the first pass of the day. *Scenically, once above the lake, there is much to be absorbed.* At clear marks on a large rock turn sharp left. *The Refuge d'Espingo is a few minutes climb to the south.* Commence the long climb, NNE at first, and then up many zigzags to the NE. Eventually, you reach...

After some stiff climbing with fine aerial views of Lac d'Oô, the route traverses high to the long ridge down to Superbagnères, with views to the Maladeta massif in Spain. The descent through the forest can be tiring, though the cable car can be taken down if required.

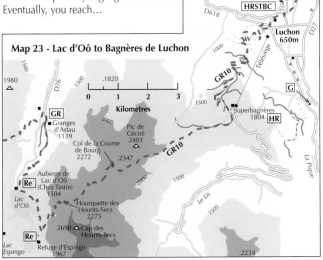

Map 23 - Lac d'Oô to Bagnères de Luchon

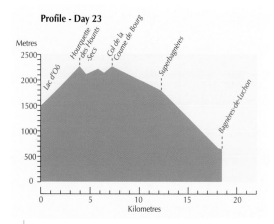

Profile - Day 23

2.10 Hourquette des Hounts-Secs, 2275m. The trail is seen clearly ahead, generally E at first, and then NE, over the first small ridge and then on to…

3.20 Col de la Coume de Bourg, 2272m. *There are tracks leading off along the ridges.* Take the waymarked one, SE, that turns to the NE, crossing the southern slopes of Pic de Céciré, with the ridge on the left. Much later the path comes onto the top of the ridge before joining a track, coming from the left. Go down this to pass an orientation table, on the right, to the road at…

4.50 Superbagnères, 1804m. *Cafés should be open and the cable car is situated to the E of the complex. It is also possible to reach the gîte, 3km S of Luchon, directly from here. There have always been warnings of getting lost on the descent along the GR10. However, it is now well marked, though forestry work may temporarily obliterate the trail. Only the start, which is not at all apparent, can be confusing.* Care is needed to get it right as maps tend to be out of date with the route that is on the ground. As the track joins the road below the orientation table, one can see an access road on the left, going to a building. Go along this road a short distance, ignoring the path to the left, going SSW, and take the obvious track going down left from the road. A little later, ignore another track going down steeply to the left, and continue down to where waymarks appear, shortly. Below there is a unique, hexagonal building. Take the path, left, in front of this building. It immediately turns back S, before continuing NW. This soon joins a track, NE, passing another on the right, before becoming a path again. Some minutes later this joins a track, E. At a track crossing, with a building ahead, turn left, N, passing a signpost a few minutes later, with a fenced enclosure on the left. A few minutes later, at another signpost, take a path N. *The old bridge here is the Viaduc du Mailhtrincat, part of the old rack railway.* Ten minutes later, the path crosses a track with a signpost, N. It joins another for a short distance and turns off right, NE, at another signpost. This becomes a wide trail for a while. Ignore a turning to the right and then ignore one to the left, near a water point. Soon, at a fork, bear left, E, and then, 10–15mins later, at a junction of paths, turn back N. Ignore paths S and NE. A few minutes later, this joins a wide trail. Turn NW and follow it to a road where you turn right, ENE. *The GR takes you into Luchon*

Lac d'Óo

centre by the main road, but the road parallel to and S
of it is quieter. Take the first right and then the next left
and follow into…

6.50 Bagnères-de-Luchon, 650m. *This is still a charming
place. There isn't a gîte in Luchon itself; the nearest one
is over 3km to the S. There are three campsites S of
Luchon, with the second one, Camping Beauregard,
probably being the best bet. Of the many hotels, La
Rencluse is reasonable and can be seen down the road
on the left just before the campsites; a sign also points
the way. It can also provide an evening meal if staying at
the campsite, though it's best to book the meal before
going on to the campsite. There is also another campsite
to the E, indicated on the sketch map. It is quieter, though
more expensive, but meals are available. However, it is a
long haul to the shops without the enticement of cafés
en route. It is here, in Luchon, that plans must be finalised
for the crossing of the Ariège.*

THE ARIÈGE

The boundaries of the Département d'Ariège are the Col
d'Auéran in the west and Col de Coma d'Anyell in the
east. However, since the food shop at Fos closed, plans
for crossing this area need to be addressed at Luchon.
The country ahead is deeply cut by north-facing and
forested valleys, making travel on foot arduous. The
weather can be more fickle than usual, and often cloud
hangs in the valleys all day. The GR10 crosses the
Département through remote territory, made even more
so since the mining industry has closed. Tourism is just
starting to bring new life to the area, its seclusion
appealing to city dwellers from the north and to those
from Spain. It takes some 15 days to cross without rest
days or days of forced idleness due to adverse weather.
A tent with cooking kit would give greater flexibility. The
following observations are made for those who would
like to reduce the amount of effort required, and are
aimed at those using the accommodation and meal services, but should also be helpful to those with camping
kit.

The problems

There are few shops from which to replenish supplies. Full rations would have to be carried all the way from Luchon for Days 27 and 28. The route imposes great physical demands; the first day to Fos is, in my opinion, the hardest on the GR10, though not statistically so. The next toughest day also occurs in this section. Only rough huts are available for accommodation from time to time. There are difficulties in navigation, due to map and guide inaccuracies. Enthusiasts have routed the GR10 through local areas of interest without gaining much eastwards distance.

The solutions

On Day 25, consider an overnight stop at the Cabane d'Uls, either using the hut or camp. This would mean an extra meal has to be carried, or use the spare one. Plan a rest day at Eylie and only carry enough daytime food for three days, bearing in mind that bread can be replenished at Fos. Carry just one lightweight evening meal for emergencies. Remember also not to arrive at Fos on Sunday or Monday, if camping and an evening meal is required. While at Eylie, preferably hitch or walk the 6km to the supermarket at Sentein. Stock up with provisions for the next two days. On Day 29, instead of climbing to Aunac, continue to the facilities at Seix. Take another rest day here as Day 30 is statistically the hardest day. Aunac can be visited, if so required, during this rest day. The next two days to St-Lizier-d'Ustou involve a long loop to the SW to pass beneath Mont Valier. This is over three times the distance and many metres of ascent more than the 10km by road. Bear this in mind if you are short of time; nevertheless, it is a fine walk and worth the effort. Reduce the workload on Day 30 by using a taxi for the road section back to the GR10, or even take it to Estours. On Day 32 there is another loop to the SE on the approach to Aulus-les-Bains. The GR10, incredibly, doesn't actually visit Aulus, though it passes only 10mins' walk away. The loop to the SE is quite a hard walk as it climbs many additional metres on the undulating descent to the Passerelle d'Ars. In fine weather it is a grand walk, passing the very impressive Cascade d'Ars, but it really should be a pleasant day walk from Aulus, unladen. There are no shops during the next six days. Also, over two days are spent negotiating loops to the south of two small towns, and if the cloud is down these loops offer little in the way of inspiration. Therefore I suggest making a base at Auzat or Vicdessos, replenishing supplies there, and negotiating these loops as day walks, using the taxi service to cover road access to the GR10. The final walk out to Mérens-les-Vals can be started at Goulier or, even better, Siguer. Meals are only available at the Refuge de Rulhe. The last two days from Siguer are quite hard and are beset with navigation problems, which it is hoped that this guide will do much to rectify.

Day 24: Bagnères-de-Luchon to Fos

Distance:	27km (16.8 miles)
Height gain:	1524m
Height loss:	1630m
Time:	9hrs 40mins
Maps:	IGN Carte de Randonnées No. 5

0.00 Bagnères-de-Luchon, 650m. From yesterday's point of arrival, take the road towards the railway station, NE. At the Casino supermarket, turn right and follow a pedestrian way beside the River l'One. At the Boulevard de Gaulle turn left over the bridge and follow the other side of the river, the left bank. Follow the trail around the E side of the airfield and small lake. At the end of the lake, bear left to join the road and turn right to Juzet-de-Luchon. Go up the steps, NNE. The path crosses the road above five times. Each time the path continues on the opposite side of the road, though sometimes it

On a fine day, the highlight must be the view S, from above Artigue. There is no gîte at this village even though one is shown on the IGN map. The final part of the descent, on an ancient paved way, is exceedingly slippery. This is a very hard day but it can be done in two stages by camping or using one of the huts.

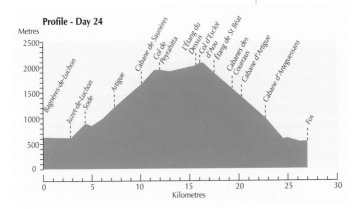

Map 24 - Luchon to Fos part one

RT
Artigue 1230m
GR10
SPAIN
2082
Ca
Col de Peyrahitta 1947
FRANCE
1888 Cabane de Saunères 1660
Sode 900m
Juzet-de-Luchon 625m
D125C
D125
Gare
D27
Luchon 650m
HRSTBC
G
0 1 2 3
Kilometres

changes direction. The sixth time that the path joins the road, turn left, N into Sode (900m). Take the left branch of the road, and at its end take the path N, ignoring another on the left and, a few minutes later, another on the left. About 10mins later, take the left branch of a fork, NNW, and follow the path to the road. Turn right and climb the road to the water point and small, covered picnic area in...

2.20 Artigue, 1230m. *There is a café/restaurant, closed Mondays, and public telephone. I met two French couples who had camped in the meadow just S of the village so it is probably all right to do so.* Go N, to the church and turn right, NW, up the road that soon becomes a track. In a few minutes take the left branch and in a further 20mins the right branch, SSE. Soon avoid two more tracks going off left, as the track turns to the S. In another 20mins, bear right, E, continuing to...

Map 24 - Luchon to Fos - part two

N125
La Garonne
1000
1000
Pic du Pouch 1473
Ca
Cabane d'Artiguessans 1025
W
La Batch
GR10
GHRTC
Gîte
Fos 544m
Ca
Cabanes des Courraus 1586
FRANCE
Pic de Burat 2154
Cabane de l'Artigue 1770
Ca 1360
Col d'Esclot d'Aou 2093
Étang de St Béat
SPAIN
L'Étang du Dessus 2018
Pic de la Hage
1000
Pic de Bacanère 2193
1445
2000
0 1 2 3
Kilometres

3.30 Cabane de Saunères, 1660m. *Not open to walkers but a nice place to sit and enjoy the views.* Take the path, NE, from the cabane and after about 15mins, three ways ahead appear. Take the left of the three, NE, and follow a long grassy crest. About 30mins later, near some rocks, take the left branch, and continue to a sign and pond at…

4.25 Col de Peyrahitta, 1947m. *There are two cabanes of the same name, down to the SE; the older of the two can be used. In good weather, a variant can be used that adds more ascent to the route by climbing to the Col des Taons de Bacanère and continuing over the pic of the same name, before joining the GR10 again. This route starts at the water trough described below, or one can climb to the ridge from this pass.* Take the path, N, to join an old track that is followed to a water point and trough. Take the centre path of the three ahead. Follow this as it contours the W side of the border ridge. About 1km later, at a junction with a hut below to the left, turn right and climb, NE. Within a few minutes take a turn to the right, SSE, following round to the NNE, to cross a rocky ridge, after which the path swings to the E.

Pic Néthou from Cabane de Saunères

Continue the long traverse of the mountainside and at a junction continue ENE. Several minutes later, cross a stream, NE, and in a few more minutes go NNE across grass to…

5.55 L'Étang du Dessus, 2018m. Go past the left of the lake and climb the clear path ahead, NNW, to the ridge at the Col d'Escot d' Aou, situated between the Pics Burat and Hage and marked by an old fence. Follow the path N, with the ridge on the left, to a point beneath Pic de Burat where the path turns back sharply, SSE at first. Ten minutes later, avoiding a turn to the right, go across grass to turn left, NW in the vicinity of Étang de St Béat. Shortly, go N, across the next patch of grass. Ignore a turning left and 10mins later continue N, and in just 2mins, the path turns to the E and then SE across grass, ignoring another path to the right. Turning to the N, the trail leads to…

7.00 Cabanes des Courraus, 1586m. *The lower one is bare and grubby, the higher is usable.* Follow the path SE, cross a stream several minutes later, and again after several minutes the path arrives at the Cabane d'Artigue. *This is also usable, with bunks and mattresses, and there is supposed to be a spring, N of the cabane.* Go past the hut for a short way before turning back to the NNW, down a wide trail into the woods, which soon joins a track. Just after the track goes round a right-hand bend, take the path left, E, which crosses another track, continuing N, to join another track. Turn left, N, and 10mins later, take the track on the right that goes down NE, to an area of tall bracken, with a hut up ahead.

7.25 Cabane d'Arteguessans, 1025m. *This is probably not available to walkers. There is a water source beside the hut.* Below the hut, at the edge of the bracken, turn right and find the path through the bracken, going E. Look out for a change of direction S, down into the wood. About 250m later turn left down an ancient, broken-paved way, beside a stream. *This is very slippery: even tungsten-tipped Leki sticks would not grip the polished slimy cobbles! Take great care and cut sticks if you do not carry them. You may also find that swarms of* *biting flies congregate at those places where exceptional care and therefore slow movement is needed and both hands are occupied! This descent is fairly steep and is about 1.4km in length. At the end, the path climbs through fallen trees, awkward to negotiate with a heavy sack, and not very welcome at the end of a long day. At the bottom, as the main path turns left, take the path, NE, ignoring another to the right and shortly, the right fork, ESE, which eventually leads down to a track beside a canal. Turn right, SE, and follow to a bridge on the left. Cross the bridge, taking the track to the main road, the N125. Turn right for a short way and then cross to go down a pleasant lane past a water point. This crosses the Garonne at…*

9.40 Fos, 544m. *The recommended gîte is on the right, just after the bridge. For the campsite, turn right at the gîte, back to the main road. Cross the road, going down the lane beside the main road-bridge to the campsite, seen on the right. As the map shows, one can approach the campsite, avoiding the lane around the N of Fos, but in heavy traffic this is unpleasant. The hotel/restaurant is to the left of the above crossing but is closed Sunday evenings and Mondays. The boulangerie is further along the main road.* **There is no épicerie now in Fos**. *If you arrive here without provisions, it will be necessary to walk or hitch to St-Béat to resupply.*

Day 25: Fos to Refuge de l'Étang d'Araing

A pleasant climb, though if the amount of climbing is intimidating, a stop at the Cabane d'Uls is a good idea. One can climb the road zigzags to Melles, but the GR takes an easy route on the other side of the valley. The European brown bear has been introduced in two places in the Pyrenees and one of these is above Fos! Travelling alone is not recommended, though many do. Only one person has been attacked, a hunter, and the bear didn't have the opportunity to talk about it. While wild camping, unidentified noises in the night seem more sinister!

Distance:	17.9km (11.1 miles)
Height gain:	1651m
Height loss:	245m
Time:	6hrs 40mins
Maps:	IGN Carte de Randonnées No. 5

0.00 Fos, 544m. From the gîte, take the road opposite, ESE. Ignore a turning left and as the lane turns to the left, take a path off right, ESE. This becomes an access road going down to the N125. Ignore the turning to Melles and continue SE along the main road past the old Customs' area where the road splits. Just before the two branches join again, take a track on the left that climbs, SSE, before turning N. Fifteen minutes later, take the left branch, E, down to the stream. Cross the stream and climb a track, then road, WNW, into…

1.10 Melles, 719m. *There is a hotel/restaurant and a van*

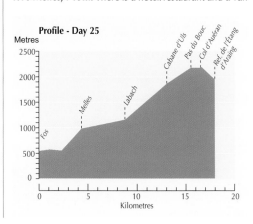

Profile - Day 25

with meat and cheese that visits Tuesdays 11.30am to 12 noon. There is a water point here and others later on, as indicated on the sketch map. Follow the road ENE, ignoring a turning to the left, for about 5km, to the scattered hamlet of…

2.25 Labach, 980m. At the car park take the concrete road on the left, and at the buildings take the path ESE. Ten minutes later ignore the path left and continue ESE, passing a water point a few minutes later. After about 30mins the path turns off sharp right, ESE. The climbing

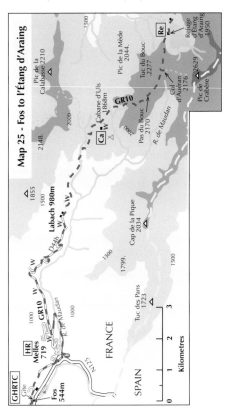

Canbane d'Uls

starts in earnest. The stream is crossed. Followed by a steep climb to a flatter area, the Plateau Marécageux (1868m). Just off the path to the SW is...

4.45 Cabane d'Uls, 1875m. *This is suitable for an overnight stop with water pipe and places to pitch a tent.* Follow the trail, SE, at first. Sometime later, ignore a path to the right, and climb S, to...

6.00 Pas du Bouc, 2170m. Cross the ridge and follow the clear path that contours the SW slopes of Tuc de Bouc. The path appears to descend a little, though the pass at the other end is supposed to be higher. Continue SE, to...

6.20 Col d'Aueran, 2176m. *Pic de Crabère is to the S and is a popular climb.* Climb the ridge to the N, for a short way to locate the descent route and then go down, E, to...

6.40 Refuge de l'Étang d'Araing, 1950m. *This is set in the impressive cirque and above the lake of the same name. There is a free hut a little way into tomorrow's stage.*

Day 26: Refuge de l'Étang d'Araing to Eylie-d'en-Haut

Distance:	7.3km (4.5 miles)
Height gain:	310m
Height loss:	1270m
Time:	3hrs 20mins
Maps:	IGN Carte de Randonnées No. 6

A much easier day today. There is a hut that can be used by walkers at the eastern end of the Mine de Bentaillou workings but due to thick cloud I was unable to identify it. The other hut there is private.

0.00 Refuge de l'Étang d'Araing, 1950m. Go down SE to pass below the dam to a path junction. Ignore the trail left, the Tour de Biros, and climb the steep slope on the other side of the gully, SE. This shortly goes past the Cabane de l'Étang d'Araing, seen on the left. Twenty minutes later take the right fork, ESE, and continue climbing, generally SE, to…
1.00 Serre d'Araing, 2221m. Turn right to the post and go down SE, turning to the WSW. The trail turns towards the E, passing a memorial after about 25mins. Continue down to…
1.40 La Mine de Bentaillou, 1870m. *The hut on the right is privately owned. There is another above open to walkers, but I was unable to locate it due to mist.*

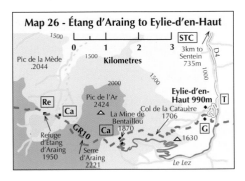

Map 26 - Étang d'Araing to Eylie-d'en-Haut

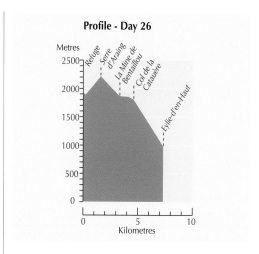

Profile - Day 26

Continue on a wide trail as it winds around the mountainside, with a track seen below. The easy walking soon ends and the path goes down right, SE, passing a small col, the Col de la Catauère (1706m) and continuing down clearly marked zigzags into the wood. Go steeply down to...

3.20 Eylie-d'en-Haut, 990m. *The gîte is one of the first houses on the right. Signs indicate the way back across a small bridge and up a grassy way to the village above, to locate the home of the guardian. The public telephone is at the S end of the lower village and it takes coins only. The guardian goes to Sentein for provisions, so a lift may be possible.*

Day 27: Eylie-d'en-Haut to Cabane de Besset

Distance:	11.5km (7.1 miles)
Height gain:	1296m
Height loss:	792m
Time:	5hrs 50mins
Maps:	IGN Carte de Randonnées No. 6

A fairly typical day in the Ariège, with another ridge to surmount, but with a cosy fire-lit evening to look forward to. Please note that if the overnight stop at Étang d'Ayes tomorrow is not suitable, then the option of the GR10E today, to the gîte at Bonac, is worth considering.

0.00 Eylie-d'en-Haut, 990m. Go down the path past the mine workings and cross the river by a footbridge. Turn right, S, along the mine track for a few metres to locate the path climbing back N, before turning to the E. Twenty-five minutes later go past a gate, and then ESE past a barn, avoiding the turning left. After climbing many zigzags through the forest and open hillside, some 90mins later, turn right, SSW, at a signpost. *The variant 10E continues straight on.* Several minutes later, cross a path, SSE, and continue to…

2.40 Col de l'Arech, 1802m. Take the path on the left, NNE, for a few minutes, before turning right, at some rocks, down a path E. This turns SSW, and then NE, before bearing right to the head of a track and…

3.10 Cabane de l'Arech, 1638m. *Available if not in use by shepherds or possibly foresters. The water source is a short way down the track on the right.* Go down the track, SW, a short way and follow it E. A few minutes later take the path on the right, going down SE. About 20mins later, at a junction, turn right, W, to cross the Arech stream. Go down SE, bearing left at a fork. The long descent through the beech wood brings you to…

4.10 Passerelle de Grauillès, 1081m. *The Cabane de Grauillès is the one seen to the S, and can be used by walkers.* Cross the bridge and take the level path on the left, N, for about 15mins. At a signpost, turn right and start the climb through many zigzags. The path enters

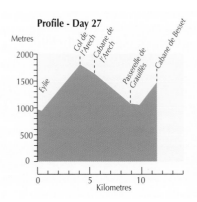

Profile - Day 27

the wood. Much later at a junction and signpost, 'Tour de Biros' again, turn left, NW, before turning back SE. Continue following the zigzags towards the NNE. Eventually, the path leaves the forest and continues climbing to...

5.50 Cabane de Besset, 1494m. *A cosy hut when the fire is lit. The water pipe in front of the cabin is no longer in use as it was severed by a fire a few hundred metres to the SE. Water has to be collected (containers in the hut) from a source about 4–5mins' walk away at the site of the fire. The flow is very slow: be prepared to wait*

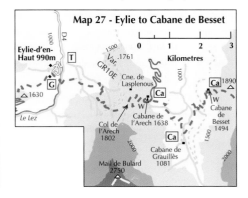

Map 27 - Eylie to Cabane de Besset

some time to fill just one jar. It is a good idea to rig some sort of support to a container to collect further supplies. Follow the faint path to the SE, which gently climbs across the slope and is marked by small cairns, and the water pipe will be seen below to the right. The pipe arrives from several hundred yards further on and investigation of the stream beds in that area didn't reveal any better flow. Any firewood that is used should be replaced from the same area.

View from Cabane de Besset to Cabane de l'Arech

Day 28: Cabane de Besset to Étang d'Ayes

Distance:	14.5km (9 miles)
Height gain:	1402m
Height loss:	1202m
Time:	7hrs 15mins
Maps:	IGN Carte de Randonnées No. 6

At the end of the day the only suitable hut with water supply is Cabane d'Aouen but this would leave an awful lot to do to reach Seix the following day. Even so, the section of this hut available for use by walkers was nearly full of building timber when I visited. This is where camping is the most viable option. However, it would be possible to use the grubby Cabane d'Eliet, just beyond the Col d'Auédole. The watercourse has dried up and has been fouled. Water would have be carried from Étang d'Ayes.

0.00 Cabane de Besset, 1494m. Take the steeply ascending path beside the SE wall of the hut and follow it to the top of the ridge called…

0.45 Clot de Lac, 1821m. *There is a hut here but no water supply. In clear weather, the next hut – the Cabane du Trapech du Milieu – can soon be seen below, and if one's legs feel up to it there is a short cut down steep grass to it. However, the GR takes a longer route to the SE.* Go E, down the gully and the path goes generally in a SE direction. About 15–20mins later there is a sharp turn to the NW, before continuing as before. Fifteen

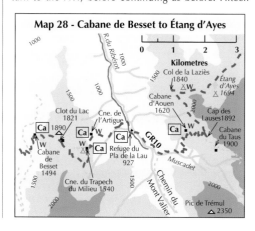

Map 28 - Cabane de Besset to Étang d'Ayes

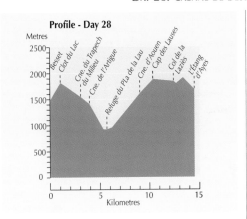

Profile - Day 28

minutes later, the trail turns back N, while another path goes straight on, to go down to…

1.30 Cabane du Trapech du Milieu, 1540m. *This hut can be used and it has a water pipe behind it.* The path starts below the hut, NNW, at first. Follow the trail down to another usable hut, the Cabane de l'Artigue, only designed for two people. The path crosses the stream and goes down its left bank to join with the Trapech Rau. The left bank of this is followed down to the valley below, which is reached at a signpost. Turn right and follow the track to a toilet block at…

2.55 Pla de la Lau, 927m. *The refuge de Pla de la Lau is in fact an unmanned and uninviting three-roomed concrete hut.* From the loos, go down to the Ruisseau du Ribérot and go across three small footbridges. Follow the path SE, to a signpost, about 10–15mins later. Turn left, E, leaving the Chemin du Mont Valier, and climb through the wood to the edge of le Muscadet stream. Many zigzags lead upward and eventually away from the stream and out of the wood. *This is a hard climb.* Eventually, a cabane can be seen a short distance down to the left…

5.10 Cabane d'Aouen, 1620m. *One small room available, with water pipe beside, though the water may need*

Étang d'Ayes

sterilising. Follow the path, ever upward, to a signpost seen high above to the E...

6.00 Cap des Lauses, 1892m. *Following the path to the SE for 500m would bring you to the Cabane du Taus but I do not know if there is a water supply there.* Turn left, N, and then NW, following the easy path, for about 2km, to...

6.35 Col de la Laziès, 1840m. Turn right, E, at the signpost and go down across open pasture. *There is a water point below to the left with a cabane in the distance, but I suspect that this is private.* Climb the short distance to the pass ahead and then descend, ESE at first, to the...

7.15 Étang d'Ayes, 1694m. *A popular spot for weekend campers. Cleaner water can be collected from the stream above the lake. It is an easy walk to the next hut, if you are without a tent, but take water with you.*

Day 29: Étang d'Ayes to Aunac

Distance:	19.6km (12.2 miles)
Height gain:	497m
Height loss:	1425m
Time:	6hrs 10mins
Maps:	IGN Carte de Randonnées No. 6

This day is described to Aunac, though most walkers will probably want to go straight on to Seix. If the weather is fine and stable, it might be a good idea to take the first part of the GR10D variant from Col d'Auédole to Pas de la Core. This was the original route but it appears that it can be too dangerous in bad weather.

0.00 Étang d'Ayes, 1694m. Cross the outlet stream and follow the trail NNE. Ten minutes later take the right fork, also NNE. Follow to the signpost on…

0.25 Col d'Auédole, 1730m. *The GR10D goes to the SE. Take the left of the two trails going in this direction.* The GR10 goes down ENE to pass the Cabane du Clot d'Eliet. Go N, and then NNW from the hut to join a track going WNW. This soon joins another where a path is found to the right, going NW. Soon, with a building on the right, take the left branch, WNW, and in a few minutes turn back sharp right, E. Ten to fifteen minutes later take a path on the left, NNE, to a track and turn right to locate the path left, N, after 50m. In a few minutes, turn off the path to another, S, ignoring another turning going SW. Follow this wide path as it traces long zigzags down to…

1.55 Étang de Bethmale, 1060m. *Access by road from Seix and Bordes-sur-Lez makes this a popular place. There are sometimes stalls selling honey and cheese. There is also a public toilet just by the GR turning to the S.* Go along the road to the E taking the higher of the two tracks beside the lake, S. Just before a building, turn left and climb steeply up through the trees for a few minutes before going N. Follow the path, above the road, turning to the S. About 40mins from the lake the path goes down to the road, which is followed SE, and then climbs to the NW. A few minutes later take the

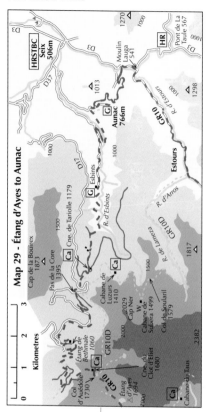

Map 29 - Étang d'Ayes to Aunac

path on the right that climbs to a track that goes S, at first, before turning NE, climbing steeply to...

3.30 Pas de la Core, 1395m. *The GR10D joins from the ridge on the right and turns back above the road.* Cross the road and go down the path NE and immediately S, that turns to the left to cross the road below. After a few minutes, take the left branch, SE, that in a few more minutes leads to a track. Turn right, SE, and more or less straight away turn left along a grassy track, E, passing the Cabane de Tariolle. About 10mins later, the track ends at a fence with buildings ahead. Turn right along a path, E, and go through a gate where the path becomes a track, to reach another gate. Follow the path E, which also becomes a grassy track, and soon turn off right at a small signpost. This grassy track soon becomes a path going down E. Twenty minutes later, pass through another gate, NE, and in 15mins you arrive at...

5.00 Esbints, 810m. *Gîte and water point.* Follow the track around the S side of the buildings to the road. Go E down the road for just under 2km and then take the track back to the right that goes down to the river. *For Seix, continue along the road, eventually ignoring turnings left then right, to the D37. Turn right and in 800m you arrive in the town centre. There is a tourist office and shops selling some mountain equipment. The two campsites are along the D17, NNE, on the E side of the*

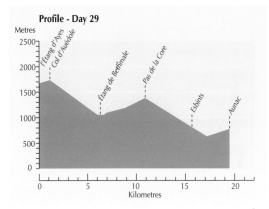

Profile - Day 29

River Salat, about 15–20mins' walk. The first is off left at a roundabout and then right along a farm track. It has a pool and the road entrance is further W, beside the public telephone. For Aunac, cross the bridge, turn left and cross another bridge, continuing E. Twenty minutes later, turn left at a junction to join the road. Turn right to a junction. The GR turns left up the track; the road goes to Aunac village; and the track on the right goes to the gîte. Turn right for the gîte at…

6.10 Aunac, 766m. *I have not visited this gîte. The GR passes around the E of the village, first passing a grassy track turning left and then one right, before coming to another sign indicating 10mins to the gîte.*

Day 30: Aunac to Rouze

This is a big day, and even further from the campsite at Seix. Please see the section on the Ariège, just before Day 24. The route takes to road and then track to Estours, continuing south-west to the valley head below the east flanks of Mont Valier. Zigzags make light work of the climb to the east, before turning north-east and then back east again to Couflens and on to Rouze.

Distance:	28.4km (17.6 miles)
Height gain:	1696m
Height loss:	1532m
Time:	9hrs 25mins
Maps:	IGN Carte de Randonnées No. 6

0.00 Aunac, 766m. From the S end of the village, go along the path to join the GR10. Take the grassy track as it winds its way down to a sharp left bend. Turn right and follow the track as it turns, S, and follow it down to the road. Turn right and follow this down to the D3. Turn right and go to…

0.40 Moulin Lauga, 541m. Turn right across the bridge and again across another to climb the road on the left bank of the Estours river. Much later the road becomes a

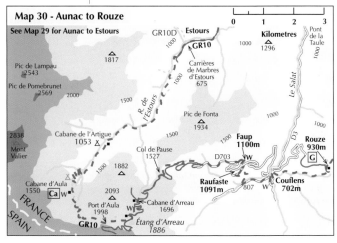

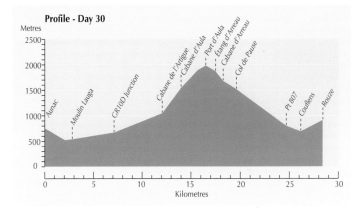

track passing buildings, above on the right, that constitute Estours. The track comes to a bridge, which is crossed, and the track the other side of the river is climbed to…

1.45 Carrières de Marbre d'Estours, 675m. *Junction of rivers and junction with GR10D, coming from the right.* Continue along the track for 10–15mins and then take a path off right that climbs the right bank of the Ruisseau de l'Estours. In a few minutes, keep to the upper path at a fork and then ignore a turning left a couple of minutes later. Ten minutes later the path turns left to join another, which is followed right, SW. Forty-five minutes later, pass through a gate and continue to…

3.15 Cabane de l'Artigue, 1053m. *Private cabin, but there is a good camping spot below.* Continue above the right bank of the river, now called the Ruisseau de l'Artigue. Much later, cross this stream by a small bridge and climb more steeply through the trees to cross grass, W, to pick up a faint path to…

4.40 Cabane d'Aula, 1550m. *Suitable for an overnight stop with the bulk of Mont Valier keeping watch.* Take the path SSE that leads to the clearly seen zigzags. Climb these and then cross the hollow, pass through a gate, to climb to…

View from Cabane de l'Artigue towards Mont Valier

5.50 Port d'Aula, 1998m. Leave the pass to the NE, taking a branch to the E. A few minutes later, take the centre path, NNE, which in 15mins leads to a forester's hut, with the Étang d'Arreau (1886m) below. Follow the track down a short distance to a short cut across the first loop. Using the short cut go across the track below, following the steep path down past a water pipe to the road again. Turn left for a few metres before turning off left, NE, and down to the private hut below, the Cabane d'Arreau (1696m). Go NE along the track ahead and turn left down a path, NE. This soon joins the track once more, which is followed to the vehicle track at...

6.55 Col de Pause, 1527m. *Actually the pass is behind the mound on the ridge ahead.* Go down the track a short way, taking the path on the left. This descends with the track on the right, which it joins later. Turn left and follow the track around a right bend. *The path turning off left at the bend used to be the way but now beehives fill the area beyond.* Continue around the bend to find another path on the left, lower down. Take this path, E, to the track once more. Turn left for 100m and then turn off left, at the bend, onto a path going E, to the track, which has now become a road, the D703. Turn left and follow the road for 15mins to a right bend. Take the track, left, E, and continue to the hamlet of Faup. The road through the hamlet forks and to the left is a water point. However, the GR turns right, back down to the D703. Turn left and then immediately right and follow this road down for a few minutes before turning sharp left onto a path, E. This turns SW, down to and across a bridge to a road at Pt 807. Turn left and follow into…

8.35 Couflens, 702m. *There are no facilities here, not even a pub! The upper part of the trail to Rouze is covered in deep mud, churned up by cattle. It is possible to avoid these sections by wading through the mud in the fields! Like the descent to Fos, biting flies, in swarms, loiter here. Be warned! There is a road and then vehicle track that goes to Rouze that takes a longer route, starting a little further on, which might be a better option after heavy rain.* Walk N along the road through the village and just past a turning on the left, go through a gate on the right, beside a house, and follow the trail upwards. As buildings appear, it is difficult to determine which might be the gîte. Bear in mind that the gîte is situated above the end of the vehicle track. Persevere to arrive at…

9.25 Rouze, 930m. *An excellent gîte d'étape. In 2001 the meals service had been discontinued as Madame Assemat was caring for her small child alone, her husband busy on the farm and no babysitters available. However, most foodstuffs were available for sale and there are complete cooking facilities in the gîte. A small contribution is requested for use of the bottled gas.*

Day 31: Rouze to St-Lizier-d'Ustou

A shorter day means a more leisurely start, with perhaps an early lunch break on the pass, admiring yesterday's descent from the Col de Pause. Should you wish to avoid the GR10 loop past the Cascade d'Ars that is scheduled for tomorrow, the two days could be combined, but the route would still take 8 hours or more.

Distance:	7.1km (4.4 miles)
Height gain:	616m
Height loss:	806m
Time:	2hrs 50mins
Maps:	IGN Carte de Randonnées No. 6

0.00 Rouze, 930m. Take the path to the left, W of the gîte and farmhouse that ascends NNW. In a few minutes turn sharply off the main path to the right, SE. Fifteen minutes later turn left, NW, past a building and then turn E. Then just follow the trail to…

1.25 Col de la Serre du Clot, 1546m. Take the lower of the two paths on the left, NE, that soon crosses a track, ENE. About 40mins later the path reaches a track. Turn right to locate the other track that is followed, E, soon taking a path on the left, N. This joins another track, near to the hamlet of Crabude. Turn left and follow this track all the way to…

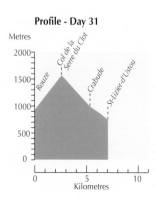

Profile - Day 31

2.50 St-Lizier-d'Ustou, 740m. *There is no gîte in this small village, but hotel/restaurant, campsite and shop, all located in close proximity. There is a gîte 2km S at Bidous. This entails a steep climb, the next day, to join the GR10 again.*

St-Lizier-d'Ustou

135

Day 32: St-Lizier-d'Ustou to Aulus-les-Bains

Today the GR10 makes a loop to the south of Aulus, climbing to Étang de Guzet, with good scenery above the tree-line and past the spectacular Cascade d'Ars. Though I expect that most walkers will be tempted to make directly for Aulus, especially if the cloud is down.

Distance:	22.5km (14 miles)
Height gain:	1361m
Height loss:	1351m
Time:	8hrs 40mins
Maps:	IGN Carte de Randonnées No. 6

0.00 St-Lizier-d'Ustou, 740m. Take the road S, through the village. Just past the last house on the right turn left over the stone bridge that was constructed by the Romans. On the other side take the ascending path ESE to Fitté (not the one left or the one going to the gîte at Bidous). About 15mins later, leave the path for a turn to the left, NE. Around 20–25mins later take the right fork, S, and in about 15mins pass the turn down right to Bidous, complete with signpost. Twenty-five minutes later embark on a series of long zigzags: the first, a sharp left turn, NNE; ignore two paths to the S, with the trail turning back to the SE; then another sharp left, NE. Ten

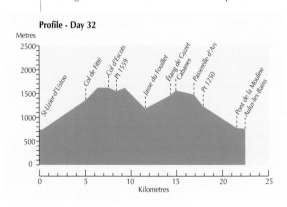

Profile - Day 32

136

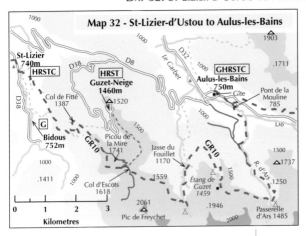

Map 32 - St-Lizier-d'Ustou to Aulus-les-Bains

minutes later, at a junction, turn right, ENE, to…

2.00 Col de Fitté, 1387m. *It is possible to reach the road below Guzet-Neige, which is seen clothing the hill to the NE, by an almost level path to the E.* Continue to the SE, and in about 50mins bear right at a fork, SSE, thus avoiding the track that climbs and passes close to the summit of Picou de la Mire (1741m). Much later the path joins a track that is followed left, ENE, then right at another track, SSE. *This track will also lead to Guzet-Neige if you turn left.* In a few minutes this leads to…

3.20 Col d'Escots, 1618m. Take the undulating path ENE and follow it down, passing Pt 1559, to reach, in about 50mins, a delightful little hanging valley, which would make an excellent camping spot. Cross the stream by the footbridge and go down NNW, ignoring a path left in 20–25mins and in another 15mins you arrive at…

4.50 Jasse du Fouillet, 1170m. *Identified by the signpost indicating a right turn for the GR10.* For Aulus, carry straight on, N, to a road that is crossed to short cut the bend. Join the road again and follow into Aulus in about 50mins. Turn right, NE, and climb through the wood, turning back towards the SSE as the path crosses the ridge. The trail passes just above…

Col d'Escots

5.45 Étang de Guzet, 1459m. *The path on the right leads down to the lake where a tent can be pitched.* Continue climbing above the NE and then E of the lake, to reach some ruined cabins. The descent, generally ESE, is another undulating type with a lot of climbing. There is still a bit of descending to do between the bridge and...

6.50 Passerelle d'Ars, 1485m. *Justifiably popular, especially at weekends.* Cross the bridge and climb NE, over the rocky prominence, following the path NNW, steeply down past the spectacular three-tier waterfall. Continue steeply downward to a track that is followed for about 10mins or so, until a path, E, can be taken. Follow this down to the N, all the way to...

8.30 Pont de la Mouline, 785m. *A short distance along the track on the other side of the bridge, the GR turns off to the right.* For Aulus, cross the bridge and follow this track NW to the road that passes to the S of the town, the D8. Cross the road and go along the lane opposite. *It is difficult to describe exactly the location of the gîte but it is in a narrow lane to the left of this one.* The other facilities are in the town below at...

8.40 Aulus-les-Bains, 750m. *The campsite is 500m N along the D32. Meals are also available at a hotel, just past la Terrasse, also on the way to the campsite.*

Day 33: Aulus-les-Bains to Mounicou

Distance:	22.3km (13.9 miles)
Height gain:	1330m
Height loss:	993m
Time:	7hrs 55mins
Maps:	IGN Carte de Randonnées No. 7

0.00 Aulus-les-Bains, 750m. Retrace your steps towards the Pont de la Mouline and take the path left, E, and then the left fork, NNE. Cross the road above, NNE, and then a right fork, SSE, 15mins later. In a few more minutes, take a left turn, NNE, and follow the path to...
2.00 Coumebière, 1400m. Cross the road, by the signpost, following the path ESE that leads to long zigzags climbing to...
3.10 Port de Saleix, 1794m. *From here a trail goes down the left side of the valley to Saleix and on to Auzat, in*

Please refer to the section on the Ariège at the end of Day 23. After days of forest and ridges, this day unfolds to grand mountain wilderness, bejewelled with lakes. The route is described to Mounicou, with the additional details on the way to Auzat and Vicdessos. Bear in mind that the next food shop on the GR10 is at Mérens-les-Vals, six days hence, and even that closes in September!

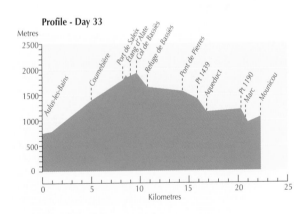

Profile - Day 33

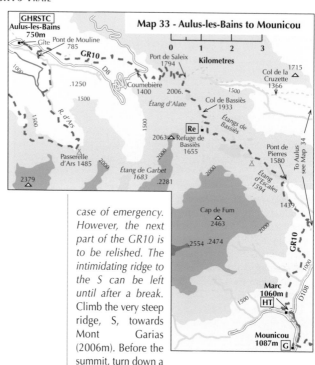

Map 33 - Aulus-les-Bains to Mounicou

case of emergency. However, the next part of the GR10 is to be relished. The intimidating ridge to the S can be left until after a break. Climb the very steep ridge, S, towards Mont Garias (2006m). Before the summit, turn down a path to the left that leaves the ridge steeply S, before easing and turning to the SE, to climb to the as yet unseen lake, the Étang d'Alate. Follow the trail around the E side of the lake and then climb easily to Col de Bassiès (1933m). *Signpost to Mounicou/Port de Saleix with the lakes and refuge seen below.* Follow the trail down the rocky slope, turning off to the right to reach the...

4.20 Refuge de Bassiès, 1655m. *This must be one of the most well-stocked refuges on the route, with even re-sealable gas cartridges available as well as some food supplies. There are many places where one could camp by the lakes below.* Either retrace your steps to the GR10 or go E, along a path, turning left between two grassy mounds to the waymarked route once more. The trail passes along the N side of the lakes until, just past Étang d'Escales, cross the stream to the right bank by a...

5.20 Pont de Pierres, 1580m. *Quite an unusually engineered stone bridge. Follow the path as it turns to the SE and go down steeply to an ancient...*

6.15 Aqueduct, 1160m. *To reach Auzat, go down the very steep zigzagging path below, generally in a SE direction and then NE down to the road, the N108. Go NE along this to the next bridge on the left. Cross the bridge and follow paths and tracks on the W side of the river until they lead back to the road again, just on the outskirts of Auzat. Follow the road around a right bend and take the next turning left to the café/bar in Auzat (728m). From the aqueduct to the bar, allow about 1hr 25mins (not the 45mins stated in the French guide). For the campsite at Vicdessos, go along the street from the bar, E, to the D108 and cross it to the road going ESE, just below the main road. This follows the river, crosses it by a bridge and continues along the right bank to the campsite at Vicdessos (708m). A footbridge crosses the*

Étang d'Alate

river into the town from the campsite. The GR10 turns right and follows the line of the aqueduct as it contours the mountainside. Above Marc it passes a tower, part of the water system; 150m later turn left. Follow waymarks down, across a road, continuing SE into the small village of Marc. *As you pass through Marc, up a narrow passage to the right you will see a sign advertising honey for sale. The owners can provide demi-pension and have accommodation in two double bedrooms. As the gîte ahead has accommodation only, it would be better to stay here, but it is more or less essential to book in advance (Tel: 05.61.64.83.86).* Continue down to the road below, turn left and cross the bridge. Either pass around the church by a path to the right, or take the track right, S, passing below a family holiday centre with public telephone inside. Continue climbing S to a road bridge on the right. Cross the bridge to the bar and book in for the gîte that is about the last building in the hamlet to the S.

7.55 Mounicou, 1087m. *I have always found this valley dank and dark, and my last visit didn't change my opinion. No food is available at the bar that seems to be run by an elderly lady, and one wonders how much longer even the gîte will survive.*

Day 34: Mounicou to Goulier

Distance:	25.3km (15.7 miles)
Height gain:	1372m
Height loss:	1349m
Time:	7hrs 45mins
Maps:	IGN Carte de Randonnées No. 7

0.00 Mounicou, 1087m. Go back across the bridge and turn right along the road a short way to a signpost. Turn left, E, and climb steeply to easier ground, with a path soon joining from the right. Continue NE/NNE to…

1.20 Refuge de Prunadière, 1614m. *A cabane that can be used as an emergency shelter with water point beside it.* Continue northwards, and about 1.5km later the path crosses the wooded ridge and starts descending the zigzags to the village below. Just above the village turn sharp left, NNW, and in a few minutes you arrive at…

2.45 Artiès, 985m. *There are public toilets and a water supply here.* Go S along the road, and 2km later, on the left, is a variant, a very steeply climbing path going to the Coumasses Grandes and junction with the GR10. *This is a short cut saving 8km (if the legs are up to it), and it is another option if visibility is poor.* Continue SSE, along the road, climbing to the right of some buildings at…

3.30 Centrale Électrique de Pradières, 1183m. As the road turns left to a car park, take the path ESE and follow to the stark buildings above…

4.40 Etang d'Izourt, 1647m. *There is a building on the left that serves as a grubby cabane for walkers. The GR10A variant goes around the E of the lake to the Refuge du Fourcat (2445m), returning at a higher level.* Climb the path on the left, NNE, and follow it to the

As can be seen from the map, Mounicou is at the end of a long loop to the south-south-west. Today, the GR10 gains height, traverses the mountainside, then drops down to Artiès before making another, even longer, loop to the south-south-east. It repeats the same scenario by doubling back high above the valley floor, before going down to Goulier. The walking itself is quite pleasant and easy – a welcome change from previous days – but if the cloud is down you can't see a thing.

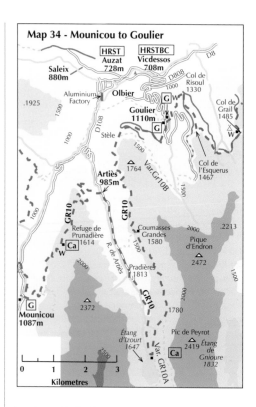

Map 34 - Mounicou to Goulier

junction with the GR10A at Pt1780. Continue N, along the contouring path. About 25mins from the lake you come to more man-made structures. Cross the concrete wall by the ladder and a few minutes later take the branch, N, at a fork and again left at another, also N. About 50mins later you arrive at the junction with the short-cut variant, seen going down NW. This is the…

6.00 Coumasses Grandes, 1580m. *Also the site of some curious stone bothies, part natural and part man-made.* Continue N, passing across a series if a rocky gullies, being much more exposed than at first seems to be the case. At a junction, there is a monument on the left at…

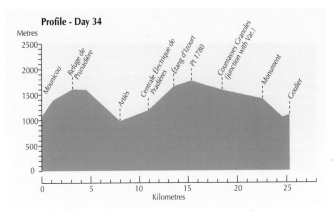

Profile - Day 34

7.05 Stèle,1410m. *The monument commemorates the opening of the Ariège GR10 on 10 October 1975 and is also the memorial to Marceau Derrieu, 1912–81, father of the GR10, who died here in the Ariège in the mountains he loved. Another variant, the GR10B, makes yet another loop to the S, starting from here.* Take the left-hand path, NNE that turns to the E, crossing a track, ENE, and joining it lower down for a few hundred metres. *This track leads to the village.* However, just after a gate, the GR takes a path left, NE, joining a narrow lane, going up into…

7.45 Goulier, 1110m. *There are two gîtes here. For the gîte Al Cantou, turn left at the top of the lane and it will be found on the left in the centre of the village. The other, the Relais d'Endron, is found at the top of the village beside the GR10 route.*

Day 35: Goulier to Siguer

Please again note comments in the section on the Ariège.

Distance:	13.2km (8.2 miles)
Height gain:	439m
Height loss:	809m
Time:	4hrs
Maps:	IGN Carte de Randonnées No. 7

0.00 Goulier, 1110m. Go up through the village past the Relais d'Endron and climb the path on the other side of the road. In 20mins this passes a spring and continues to a signpost at the Col de Risoul. Turn right, SSW, along a track. *A short cut avoids the corner to the track but misses the signpost.* At this point turn ESE, and then SSE along a path just above and to the left of the track. Follow it until the junction with the GR10B where you turn NE on a path to...

Goulier, Olbier and Auzat

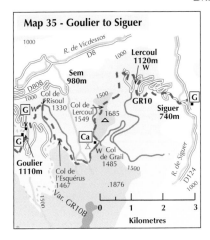

Map 35 - Goulier to Siguer

1.20 Col de l'Esquérus, 1467m. Take the path SE. About 20mins later it turns to the E and crosses a stream before joining the track that comes from the Col de Risoul. Turn right, E, and follow the track to a barrier. Pass the barrier to…

1.55 Col de Grail, 1485m. *To the left there is a forester's hut that is available to walkers. To the right there is a water point and it would be possible to camp.* Take the

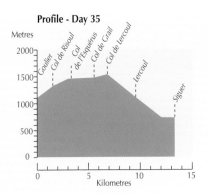

Profile - Day 35

track, WNW, that goes past another barrier beside the hut. Follow this for a few minutes before talking a path right, NE. Follow this to the wooded pass on the N ridge of Pic de la Bède at…

2.20 Col de Lercoul, 1549m. Follow the path down, NNE, and 25 mins later this joins a track at a signpost. Turn left, NNW, following the track round a bend to the right and take the path off E, at another signpost. This comes down to a road, which is followed to the right, SSW. Five minutes later take a path S, which crosses the road and enters the upper road of the village. Turn left then right to the centre of…

3.05 Lercoul, 1120m. *There is a water point here.* The GR does not follow the road, as in the French guide, but goes down a path, starting on the right just N of the centre. This goes down to the S, to pass a track on the left, coming from a bend in the road, and continues descending to the E, taking the left branch at a fork. About 20–25mins later the path crosses the road, E, and in a few minutes joins it. Turn left NE and follow it round to the SE, over a bridge, past the church and ENE up to…

4.00 Siguer, 740m. *I have marked the map as though there is a gîte here, but that is not entirely true. The villagers have set aside a room in a courtyard for walkers, free of charge. There are bunks, tables, chairs, a fridge, washing facilities and a shower, but no cooking facilities. Without the latter it cannot truly be described as a gîte, but compared with some of the mountain cabanes it is luxurious!*

Day 36: Siguer to Refuge de Clarans

Distance:	18.7km (11.6 miles)
Height gain:	1657m
Height loss:	1297m
Time:	8hrs 55mins
Maps:	IGN Carte de Randonnées No. 7

This is a hard day, and the route does not follow maps and guides in several places. These are noted in the text. Low cloud could make navigation very tricky.

0.00 Siguer, 740m. From the gîte and courtyard, go up E between the buildings to cross the road above and then, a little later, cross it again, ESE. After more steep climbing, cross a track, NNE, and enter...

0.30 Gestiès, 960m. *There is a telephone and water point.* Go up to the right of the church and avoid two turnings to the left and continue E. Carefully follow the marks and narrow path up to...

1.35 Col de Gamel, 1390m. *I have not yet met anyone who has actually found the correct route onto the ridge above. Bear in mind that the next objective is the Pla de*

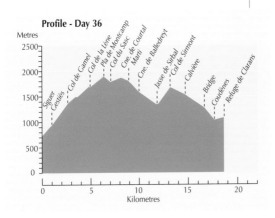

Profile - Day 36

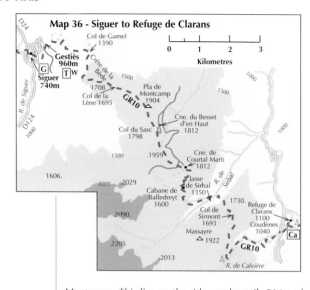

Map 36 - Siguer to Refuge de Clarans

Montcamp. This lies on the ridge and entails 514m of ascent. I think that the problem is exacerbated by new trees growing over an area that is clear on the map. Ignore the path ahead and turn right, S. Climb the clear track, well-used by cattle. As it levels out, waymarks are still visible; keep a sharp eye on the left for the route up the first grassy ridge coming down from the main ridge above, the Crête de la Bède. Do not go too far along the level track as this will contour to another ridge coming down the mountain and eventual confusion. If no route is spotted, then climb the best way to the main ridge. Higher up the convex slope the waymarks are quite clear. Follow the marks over a high spot and down to Col de la Lène (1695m). Climb the ridge ahead, ESE to SE. Continue SE across the summit plateau, passing two poles, as the trail passes just below the summit rocks of…

3.55 Pla de Montcamp, 1904m. Go down S, and quickly the waymarking becomes frequent all the way to the Col du Sasc (1798m). *The shepherd's hut of Besset d'en Haut* *is seen below to the NE, beside the track.* Go S from the signpost and follow the clear trail climbing to a rough plateau. Here, post markers are followed SE, SSE and then E until the hut can be seen below. It is Cabane de Courtal Marti (1812m). *The GR from here does not follow that shown in the French guide.* Go SSE to the rocks on the plateau horizon and then SSW to some others, from which the path works its way steeply down through heather. *Take care, as the slightest slip can cause broken branches to rip one's legs!* This path zigzags down to Cabane de Balledreyt (1600m), which now is a ruin. *It is a little awkward finding the way to the stream S of the cabin.* Follow the path away from the cabin, SE, and in 100m turn right, SSW, then left, SE, and finally SSW through some reeds to pass through rocks.

Continue following the path along the stream and soon cross it. Follow the path down to...

5.55 Jasse de Sirbal, 1350m. *This open area is deeply rutted by much cattle use and it would be nigh impossible to camp here comfortably.* Waymarks indicate that the bridge should not be crossed. The GR climbs from the Jasse from the NE corner. Turn left through the bushes, before the bridge, and try to follow a trail on the left of the stream. At the end of the clearing, cross the stream and find the path in the corner. Climb steeply though the trees to the pass, clear of the trees, at...

6.55 Col de Sirmont, 1693m. Depart to the S, go down steeply into the woods and continue following the trail S. *It appears that the French guide is wrong again as, according to the compass, the trail continues S, until a clearing at the Ruisseau de Calvière. A nice spot for a camp.* Turn sharp left, N, and in about 10mins the trail crosses a bridge. Descending E now, and 40mins after the last bridge, another is crossed and then a few minutes later, the path comes to the road at...

8.40 Coudènes, 1040m. Cross the road bridge and go up the track NNE. Just past a stream, the GR turns right but continue N into a clearing and on the left, halfway across, is the small hut of...

8.55 Refuge de Clarans, 1100m. *Camping is possible beside the hut, though a better place is in another pasture above. Water, of the brown variety, can be collected from the streams either side, but a little further N is the stream coming from the Plateau de Beille. The cabane is small and some of the bed planks have been removed – probably vandalised for firewood!*

Day 37: Refuge de Clarans to Refuge du Rulhe

Distance:	18km (11.2 miles)
Height gain:	1626m
Height loss:	541m
Time:	8hrs
Maps:	IGN Carte de Randonnées No. 7

0.00 Refuge de Clarans, 1100m. *The GR passes NE of the clearing but the meadow will probably be very wet. It is possible to wander off on farmers' trods on the first climb so don't go too far without confirming marks.* Retrace one's steps to the stream and turn left up the waymarked path. The undergrowth is dense, but the way clear enough. Just over 1 hour later, at a junction, turn NE. *The next part of the climb is very steep and must be awkward in wet conditions.* Higher up, two signposts are passed, both times NNE. As the gradient eases, high bracken and then broom encroach on the path for

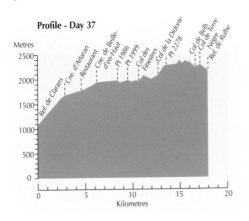

Profile - Day 37

Grand scenery unfolds as height is gained. This is another hard day, but with a tent there is no problem as there are suitable places to camp. Traditionally, a long descent to the Cabane de Rieutort could be made. The new hut on the opposite side of the ridge, the Cabane d'Embizon, could be used, but viewing it from the ridge on my last visit it seemed to be occupied by a shepherd, with people camping in tents nearby. Appearing almost as a mirage or a space-station is the large restaurant complex on the Plateau de Beille. Quite incongruous, though welcome, it is open for snacks and meals and there are picnic tables outside.

Andorran peaks from the Plateau de Beille

a short distance and before it emerges onto open hillside. Soon turn N to the...

1.55 Cabane d'Artaran, 1695m. *This cabane can be used though it is about 12mins to the ample water supply to the NNE.* Go NE to the track that starts just beyond the hut. Follow this NNE, crossing the stream and on to...

2.20 Centre d'Accueil du Plateau de Beille, 1817m. *Superb view to the mountains N of Andorra.* The route ahead differs from the French guide and some maps. South of the restaurant there is a noticeboard and three tracks. The one on the right is the one that we arrived on. The centre one goes S. Take the one on the left, that climbs SE. This reaches a junction where the central track also arrives. Leave the two tracks on the right and take the one going E, which winds to the S to...

3.00 Cabane de Beille-d'en-Haut, 1939m. *Again the route is incorrect in the French guide.* Go S a short way from the hut and at the junction, instead of turning left, go straight on, with a red paint arrow indicating the way and waymarks appearing shortly. *The GR now follows* *vehicle tracks in the grass to a point above Finestres.* About 20 mins later, as the main track bears left after a small hill on the right, go SSE up a grassy track to the top of the next hill (Pt 1986). Go down to the hollow and follow the track

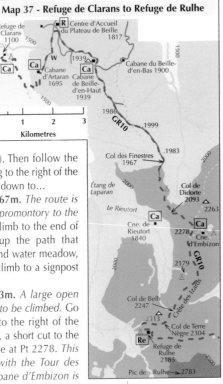

Map 37 - Refuge de Clarans to Refuge de Rulhe

over the next hill (Pt 1999). Then follow the track to the next hill, passing to the right of the summit (Pt 1983), and then down to...

4.15 Col des Finestres, 1967m. *The route is seen climbing to the rocky promontory to the S.* Follow the track S and climb to the end of the vehicle tracks. Pick up the path that wanders across a hollow and water meadow, *suitable for camping,* and climb to a signpost and...

5.10 Col de Didorte, 2093m. *A large open convex slope to the SE has to be climbed.* Go ESE at first, climbing just to the right of the escarpment. Nearer the top, a short cut to the right can be taken, to arrive at Pt 2278. *This would miss the junction with the Tour des Montagnes d'Ax. If the Cabane d'Embizon is required, it is necessary to keep to the edge to locate the best way down.* Continue S, passing just to the right of the rocky crest, to reach a small pass with the steep conical mountain ahead and a small étang below to the right that is easy to reach for a camp. *From the étang, one can climb back to the GR on a line to the S.* Climb steeply up the rocky ridge until a traverse right can be made that leads to the Crête des Izards. *A tiring traverse towards the end of a long day.* Continue along the grassy ridge to...

7.25 Col de Belh, 2247m. *The GR10 used to turn down left here, before the building of the refuge ahead. From*

The old GR10 trail below Col de Beil with Pic de Rulhe beyond

the signpost, take the path S, which turns to the SW, gently climbing to the Col de Terre Nègre (2304m). Go down WSW to…

8.00 Refuge de Rulhe, 2185m. *Camping is also allowed close by.*

Day 38: Refuge de Rulhe to Mérens-les-Vals

Distance:	12.6km (7.8 miles)
Height gain:	437m
Height loss:	1572m
Time:	5hrs
Maps:	IGN Carte de Randonnées No. 7

Again, the French guide shows the route incorrectly around Étang Bleu and on the descent from the Crête de la Lasse. A large boulder field has to be crossed, followed by a stiff climb, before the long walk out to the Ariège valley.

0.00 Refuge de Rulhe, 2185m. Follow the trail to the E, climbing to the left side of the obvious pass ahead. Ten minutes after leaving the refuge, use the left fork, ENE, and in another 20mins you arrive at the Col des Calmettes (2318m). Go E, down into boulder country. The GR passes N of the first small tarn, though the S side is probably quicker, and then climb to a point above the **S** of the Étang Bleu. From here, continue climbing boulders, turning towards the NE, until the trail leads to a

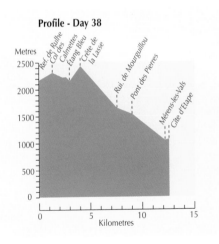

Profile - Day 38

157

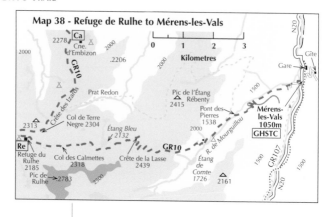

Map 38 - Refuge de Rulhe to Mérens-les-Vals

steep ridge, coming down from the right. Climb steeply to the top of the ridge and then right to...

Looking back along the Ruisseau de Mourguillou

2.15 Crête de la Lasse, 2439m. *As mentioned above, the route differs from that shown and now turns to the S.* Go NE for a short distance to a sharp turn right, S, down zigzags to the valley floor. Follow marks to the E.

Above the Étang de Comte, the trail turns NE, passing above some crags, before taking to more zigzags which lead down to the Ruisseau de Mourguillou. Follow the path down the left bank until a crossing can be made at…

4.00 Pont de Pierres, 1538m. Ten minutes later the path crosses a track, NNE, and joins it below. Turn right and after two bends of the track, at a signpost, turn left, W. The trail turns to the NE and about 35–40mins later it joins the road, which is followed E into…

5.00 Mérens-les-Vals, 1050m. *For the gîte, climb the road under the railway tracks, E. It turns left over a stream, where the GR turns right. Follow the road N, then E to the gîte. There are also rooms available at the hotel/bar, but no meals except breakfast. A small shop on the main road sells provisions but closes for holidays in September. There is a campsite 10 minutes S, with a small shop.*

Day 39: Mérens-les-Vals to Refuge des Bésines

From now on, daily accommodation returns and the daily workload reduces. Heat might well be a problem nearer the coast, when adequate water supplies are an imperative. Today, it is back to the high mountains again.

Distance:	9.5km (5.9 miles)
Height gain:	1367m
Height loss:	313m
Time:	4hrs 20mins
Maps:	IGN Carte de Randonnées No. 8

0.00 Mérens-les-Vals, 1050m. From the gîte, go SE, back to the stream in its water channel. Turn left up the path, E, which becomes a track that crosses a road, continues slightly to the left and passes by the ancient church to the road again. Follow this a short way until about 100m past the bridge over the Redon, turn left, E, at a signpost, turning right, ESE, at the junction. Climb the path on the right bank of the Nabre all the way to a footbridge that leads to the left bank. Continue climbing to...

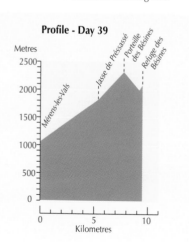

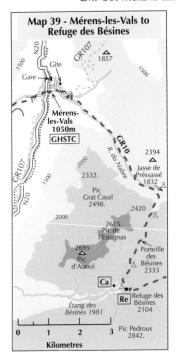

Map 39 - Mérens-les-Vals to Refuge des Bésines

2.20 Jasse de Préssassé, 1832m. Here the trail turns to the S and then SSW. After a steep but short climb it arrives at the picturesque and small Lac d'Etagnas (2056m). Another stiff but short climb leads to...

3.40 Porteille des Bésines, 2333m. The refuge can be seen below through the trees. Go W at first, and then continue descending, generally SSW. Take care lower down as the trail turns SSE and wanders around various obstacles, losing sight of the refuge for a time before climbing the short distance to the...

4.20 Refuge des Bésines, 2104m. *There is a small place to camp beside the hut and a cabane by the lake.*

*Refuge des Bésines
and Pic Pedrous*

Day 40: Refuge des Bésines to Refuge des Bouillouses

Distance:	18km (11.2 miles)
Height gain:	602m
Height loss:	696m
Time:	5hrs 50mins
Maps:	IGN Carte de Randonnées No. 8

Another super high mountain day with a choice of three equally good places to stay, the cheapest being the auberge. There are many good suitable spots until Lac des Bouillouses.

0.00 Refuge des Bésines, 2104m. Take the path, ESE, from the refuge for just a few metres and then leave the clear path ahead for a sharp turn down right, W, that turns to the E. Follow this path up the valley. In about 20mins there is a junction with a signpost. Take the left path, NNE, of the two going northwards. About 40mins from the refuge the trail crosses a stream and several minutes later turns sharp right, S, leaving the path straight ahead, before continuing NNE. Go past a small lake and follow the route around boulders to…

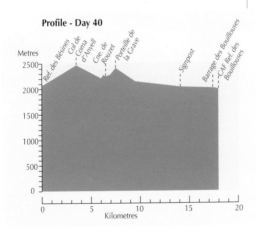

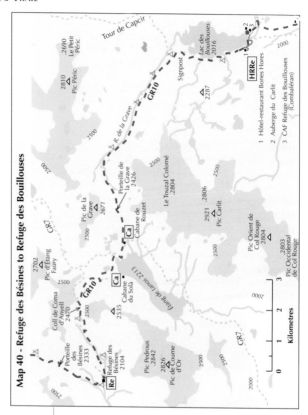

Map 40 - Refuge des Bésines to Refuge des Bouillouses

1.40 Coll de Coma d'Anyell, 2470m. Take the path ENE from the signpost and a few minutes later, at another signpost and junction with the GR7, take the right fork, SSE. About 15mins later, at another junction, turn left, NE. *The other path, perhaps, goes to the small hut, the Cabane du Solà on the N edge of the Lanos lake.* The trail wanders, generally SE, to a signpost above the large Étang de Lanos. *This signpost doesn't actually indicate the direction of the GR10, only the GR7!* Follow the clear path going up S, not the waymarks going N. The path turns E to climb over a low ridge to a grassy patch. Go straight across the grass to find waymarks that lead to the hut below, the Cabane de Rouzet. *The Porteille de la Grave can be clearly seen ahead.* Follow the path, E from the hut, to…

3.10 Porteille de la Grave, 2426m *('Grava' on maps with Catalan spelling).* Go down E from the pass. The trail passes a small lake and a little later crosses the stream below by a small bridge. Ignore a path going off left and, shortly afterwards, one going right. The trail now takes a SE direction, along the right bank of the Ruisseau de la Grave. About halfway along the valley ignore a path left and much later the path comes to a…

4.50 Signpost, 2050m. The trail turns S along the W side of Lac de Bouillouses. A few minutes later ignore a path left but continue SW, and shortly another signpost indicates S again. Continue along the popular trail to a track, with the hotel/refuge/restaurant appearing on the right. Cross the dam and follow the road down, first passing the auberge on the left and then, also on the left…

5.50 CAF Refuge des Bouillouses (Refuge Combaléran), 2010m. *The three places of accommodation are listed and their locations marked on the sketch map.*

Étang de Lanos and the Carlit

Day 41: Refuge des Bouillouses to Planès

A long walk out through the Bolquère forest to the east end of the high plateau of the Cerdagne. Care needed in the initial section if it is misty.

Distance:	18.2km (11.3 miles)
Height gain:	167m
Height loss:	677m
Time:	4hrs 35mins
Maps:	IGN Carte de Randonnées No. 8

0.00 CAF Refuge de Bouillouses, 2010m. Go SE down the road from the CAF refuge for about 500m. Turn right across a footbridge and take the path SW, not those going S or W. Five minutes later fork left S and then fork right, SW, turning S again. A few minutes later, fork left S and 10mins later pass a signpost, seen below to the right, before arriving at a wooden hut, Cabane de l'Étang de la Pradeille (1950m). Take the path E that becomes a track, and at a junction continue along the track ESE,

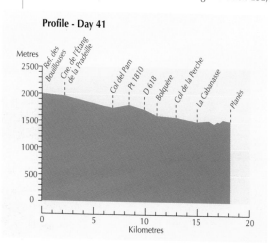

Profile - Day 41

ignoring the path left. Ten minutes later continue E, ignoring a path right, at a signpost. *The track becomes too rough for vehicles after a while but continues as a track most of the time.* Fifteen to twenty minutes later, at another signpost, ignore the path off left and continue SSE, crossing a wide ski piste and passing under cables. The GR arrives at a track on the left and immediately turns off to the right SE to arrive at another junction, the...

1.35 Col de Pam, 1750m. Go straight up the track ahead, SE. Thirty minutes later go straight across a junction, SE again. A few minutes later the track turns right where the third path on the right is taken SSW, just after the bend. A few minutes later, cross another track at a

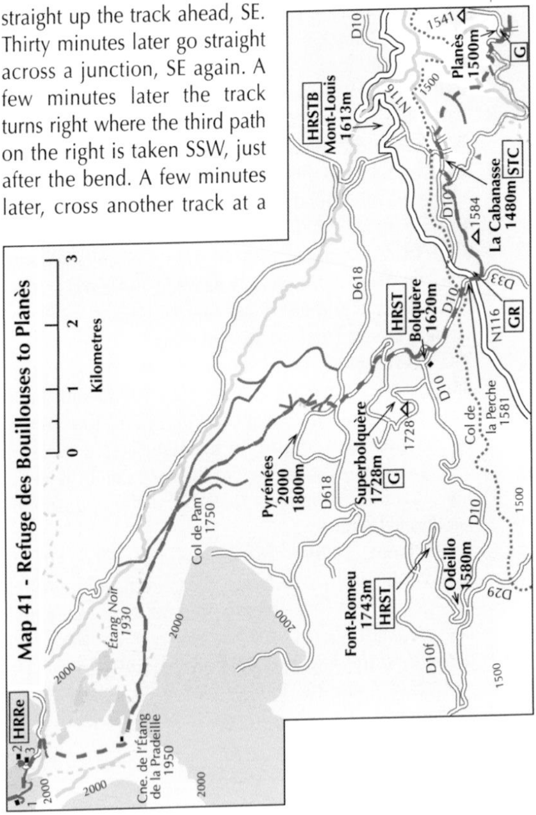

Map 41 - Refuge des Bouillouses to Planès

junction, continuing SSW on a path to the road coming down from Pyrénées 2000. Turn left to the crossroads with the D618. Cross the road and go S down the D10 road opposite. After 1km take the path on the right that cuts across a long loop of the road. At the road again, turn right, W. *Another short cut can be made to the left, just before a house.* Follow the road down to a left fork into…

2.45 Bolquère, 1620m. *Hotel/restaurants and shop that can be seen on the upper road to the right.* Upon reaching the D10, turn left and follow SE, eventually crossing the track of the 'Little Yellow Train' and on to the N116 at the…

3.10 Col de la Perche, 1581m. *Opposite and to the left is the Relais les Melezes with gîte and restaurant.* Cross the N116 and go along the road to the right of the relais. Take the track on the left, E, beside a wood and follow all the way to a road with a sign indicating camping at 400m. Turn left and follow into…

3.40 La Cabanasse, 1480m. *There is an important épicerie here as the next is at Py in three days' time. Please note that it closes on Tuesdays!* Go through the village, pass a road on the right and then take a path SSE. A few minutes later it crosses a track, SSE, and about 15mins further on it passes a track to the right and climbs to a road. Turn right to another road and turn left, E. Follow this road around to the right and down to a bridge over the stream. Ignore the road climbing to the right and follow the level road to the gîte opposite the telephone booth at…

4.35 Planès, 1500m. *The new and excellent gîte, Le Malaza, is run by two ladies, who are usually present during the day. Their telephone number is available if not. Breakfast is left as self-service, so an early start can be made if the next two days are planned as one. The gîte at La Cassanya is now closed, as is the Centre Bethany.*

Day 42: Planès to Refuge du Ras de la Carança

Distance:	14.8km (9.2 miles)
Height gain:	1168m
Height loss:	837m
Time:	5hrs 15mins
Maps:	IGN Carte de Randonnées No. 8

0.00 Planès, 1500m. Go up the track on the W side of the gîte that climbs ESE to the road above. Climb past the church, ignoring a road on the right. *The GR used this road from the bridge before the new gîte opened.* Shortly take the path on the left, E, that comes to a track. Turn right to a junction and opposite there is a path climbing S. Take this to another track and turn left, ESE. This takes 10–15mins from the gîte. About 15mins later, the track reaches another junction where a path S is taken to join the track above. Turn left, SSE and follow

The next three days link the Carlit and Canigou mountain groups. Probably due to new tracks being cut in the woods, it is reported that some walkers are getting lost above the village. Care is therefore needed. The next two days can be done in one but only with an early start and some swift walking.

Profile - Day 42

169

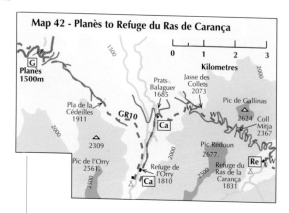

Map 42 - Planès to Refuge du Ras de Carança

this track. About 25mins later, ignore a track climbing to the right but continue SE along the level track that becomes a path and at a junction turn right, SE to the...

1.15 Pla de Cédeilles, 1911m. *An open grassy area.* Follow the path and in 10mins it passes a water point. In another 10mins it turns NE, where a track goes off right. The path leads down to the stream and gently climbs SSW to a stone shelter or 'orry'. Just past this, cross the bridge on the left and turn left, N, ignoring another path that goes down to the left. The path shortly arrives at...

2.15 Refuge de l'Orry, 1810m. *A cabane used by farmers but also suitable for an overnight stay by walkers.* Go N and in a few metres a track begins and is followed N to a junction. Take the right fork up to another usable cabane at the...

2.45 Prats Balaguer, 1685m. Just past the hut, take the path right, SE. About 40mins later, the path passes a water point, the Font dels Collets, before joining a track. Go right, NNE, to another and turn right, SE. A few minutes later, take a path off left, ENE, which turns SE. In about 15 minutes it passes a water point, and then crosses the track to the ESE some 10mins later. Within a few minutes the path joins the track where one turns right, S, for a few metres to find the path on the left

Ras de la Carança

going SSE. At the next track, turn left to find the path going E. Cross the track once more, E, before arriving at...

4.25 Coll Mitja, 2367m. The descent from the pass takes a direct line down the steep slope crossing the track below many times. Some of these short cuts are clearly marked, but towards the bottom they are not. The track can be followed but it would add greatly to the distance. The line is generally a little N of SE. Towards the bottom of the slope the track is followed SW to...

5.15 Refuge du Ras de la Carança, 1831m. *Open all year but guardian only present during the summer. No showers are available so one has to make one's own arrangements.*

Day 43: Refuge du Ras de la Caraça to Mantet

Distance:	11km (6.8 miles)
Height gain:	591m
Height loss:	887m
Time:	4hrs
Maps:	IGN Carte de Randonnées No. 8

The municipal gîte has closed due to fire. There are presently three places to stay in Mantet; it would be a good idea to book in advance as this is a popular location. One gîte does not appear in the Cimes-Pyrénées list: Chez Richard (Tel: 68 05 60 99. Email: richard.cazenove@wanadoo.fr).

0.00 Refuge du Ras de la Caraça, 1831m. Go S to the signpost and cross the bridge. Go up the grassy track SE, then E. About 15mins later take a left-hand fork in the path, E. At the water meadow of Pla de Bassibès, bear left a little to find marks across the grass. The path turns to the N, then NE, gradually descending before turning to the right and SE for the climb to the pass. At a ruined cabin cross the grass SE to locate the path. Much later, pass through a gate while the path is going NE and a few minutes later, leave it on another to the SE. This turns NE again climbing steeply to…

1.50 Coll del Pal, 2294m. *The Réserve Naturelle de Mantet starts here.* From the pass the GR can be seen contouring the slope to the SE. Follow this but be careful to spot the right turn SE up rocks, when passing through

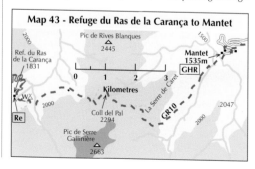

Map 43 - Refuge du Ras de la Caraça to Mantet

a small section of trees. *The clear
path going straight on will eventually come to the grassy ridge at
Pt 2274, well below the correct
spot!* Post markers lead the way
above to a large cairn at the…

2.30 La Serre de Caret, 2300m.
Go SE across the grass to the very
steep descent, ESE from La Serre
de Caret. Once past the steep
part, from a signpost to Mantet,
follow the path NE towards the village. Just before the
flat area below the village, turn down right to cross a
bridge, turning NNE. A few minutes later, cross another
bridge to climb the steep cobbled lane into…

*The Canigou massif
from the Coll del Pal*

4.00 Mantet, 1535m (at the first gîte). *The first place to
stay is on the left of the first steep lane into the village,
which is Chez Richard. Richard Cazenove and his wife
Angeline run the chambre d'hôtel and gîte with full meals
service. The next place to stay is the auberge/restaurant
at the top of the village, on the left, just after the road has
turned left. From here, above to the right and E is La
Cavalle, an equestrian centre with a gîte.*

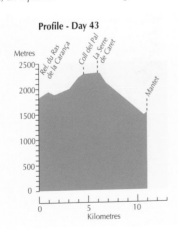

Profile - Day 43

173

Day 44: Mantet to
Refuge de Mariailles

The shop at Py is the last for three-and-a-half days. At Mariailles, high and rocky mountains return.

Distance:	14.5km (9 miles)
Height gain:	1030m
Height loss:	847m
Time:	5hrs 05mins
Maps:	IGN Carte de Randonnées No. 10

0.00 Mantet, 1535m. Go up through the village past the auberge and take the road on the right that goes E to La Cavalle. Find the path on the left that climbs NE beneath the power lines. It meets the road about 15mins later and immediately continues the zigzags to the road again at…

0.30 Col de Mantet, 1761m. Go down NE to reach the road about 25mins later. *It is possible to follow the road but the GR soon takes to a path.* After 300m take the path down E and 10mins later, join the road for a short distance and take a path SSE. Within a few minutes it passes a water point and the Méridienne Verte post. *This*

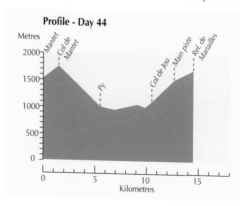

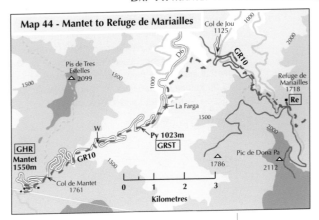

Map 44 - Mantet to Refuge de Mariailles

marks the year 2000 tree-planting effort along the meridian through Paris. *Cross the road E and then again E. In 10mins cross the road again, ENE, taking the road opposite into…*

1.50 Py, 1023m. *There is a gîte here and bar/restaurant with shop beneath. Ask at the bar for the shop to be opened.* From the bar, take the lower road E. A few minutes later, this becomes a track for a short way before joining a road, the D6. Turn left, NE, and at a signpost take the narrow road on the right, NNE, cross a bridge and continue NNE. After 500m, just past the hamlet of La Farga, ignore the first path right and take the next path climbing N. Fifteen minutes later ignore a path left, and much later the path crosses the ridge, turning SE. In 1km it arrives at…

3.25 Col de Jou, 1125m. Turn right and climb the steep track beyond the notice board that starts S and crosses over a stream E. Twenty minutes later the track becomes a path passing by a bend in the main track. After another 25 minutes the path joins the track, which is followed S. *Do not take the path opposite and slightly to the right.* Within a few minutes take a path on the left, S. *The track will lead to the refuge but it is very dusty and busy. The French guide describes the path route but shows the GR* *on the track.* Soon ignore a path ascending right and within a few minutes the path follows the left edge of a watercourse. *Very pleasant compared with the track!* Fifteen minutes later leave the watercourse on the path N that leads to the track, which is followed NE to...

5.05 Refuge de Mariailles, 1718m. *A popular spot with access by track, set upon a rocky promontory.*

Day 45: Refuge de Mariailles to Chalet-Hôtel des Cortalets

Distance:	17.3km (10.8 miles)
Height gain:	990m
Height loss:	558m
Time:	5hrs 40mins
Maps:	IGN Carte de Randonnées No. 10

The route today climbs to about 2000m, and makes a long traverse of the Canigou massif before climbing the ridge to the north to reach the refuge. It is possible to climb over the top of the Canigou from this traverse, following a clear path. From the top, a path also leads to the refuge

0.00 Refuge de Mariailles, 1718m. From the refuge, go SSE up the path leading to the track above and water channel. Ignore the track to the left going to a cabin but take the path immediately below the water channel, S. This leads to a stream where the path turns N. Some minutes later, while the path travels E, it passes through

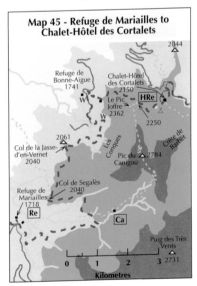

Map 45 - Refuge de Mariailles to Chalet-Hôtel des Cortalets

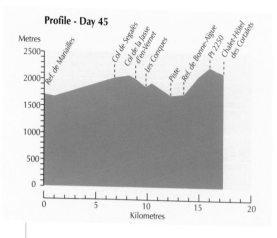

Profile - Day 45

a gate. Thirty-five minutes later the path crosses another stream and climbs to the N. Ignore a path left before arriving at the junction with the path to the Canigou. *Follow the yellow waymarks for the Canigou.* Continue W, cross another stream and follow the path to...

2.15 Col de Segalès, 2040m. Ignore the path going down left as your path turns to the N. again. Thirty minutes later the path arrives at a sign where it goes down E at the Col de la Jasse-d'en-Vernet. Follow the path down to Les Conques, an open, steep and rocky area much devastated by avalanches. *Care is needed crossing Les Conques to gain the far side of the ravine, which it descends before climbing again.* Follow the trail up through the rocks, marks and cairns and then turn left to pass beneath a rocky outcrop. Pass a water point and go down the right side of the ravine before turning towards the N, then W and on to a track. Turn right, NNW and follow to...

4.05 Refuge de Bonne-Aïgue, 1741m. *This is a usable cabane but the water supply can dry up in the height of summer.* Follow the track to the E for about 50m and take the path climbing to the right, ESE. At a clearing the path passes an orry and continues to climb more easily

*A glance back to the
Refuge de Mariailles*

to the N in order to cross the NW ridge of Le Pic Joffre.
Follow the path ESE to the pass on the NE ridge at...
5.20 Pt 2250m. Turn left and follow the highway down
to the left side of the lake and on to...
5.45 Chalet-Hôtel des Cortalets, 2150m. *The chalet has
room accommodation and the building to the left
contains the dormitory. It is open from the end of June
to the end of September. Full meals service is available
and camping permitted by the small lake. It might be a
good idea to book in advance at weekends. The
unguarded refuge remains open all year. The Canigou
(2784m) is an easy summit from here and vehicle access
by track makes it very popular.*

Day 46: Chalet-Hôtel des Cortalets to Mines de Batère

Distance:	16.8km (10.4 miles)
Height gain:	273m
Height loss:	923m
Time:	4hrs
Maps:	IGN Carte de Randonnées No. 10

It is customary to descend to Arles-sur-Tech on this stage, but accommodation there is very limited. Stopping at the gîte at the Mines allows an early morning ascent of the Canigou, if so desired, before starting for the Mines. Plenty of cheaper accommodation can be found by walking or catching the bus to Amélie-les-Bains.

0.00 Chalet-Hôtel des Cortalets, 2150m. *The start of the GR is not too clear.* Go behind the chalet, the E side, and cross the open area to the N to locate the path descending steeply N. This joins the vehicle track, which is followed N to an area known as the Ras dels Cortalets. Signpost and main track turns left. Take the track on the right, SE, and follow down several kilometres to a junction at...
0.55 Ras de Prat Cabrera, 1739m. *Signpost where the track turns left and a path goes straight on.* Turn right

Profile - Day 46

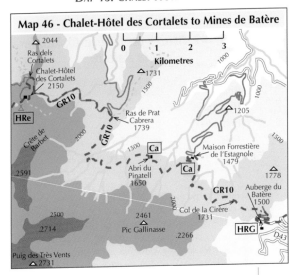

Map 46 - Chalet-Hôtel des Cortalets to Mines de Batère

down a path, SW, that eventually crosses three streams as it turns to the E. Half an hour or so after these, a rough wooden hut is reached, the…

1.55 Abri du Pinatell, 1650m. *Five minutes along the path is a stream.* Continue along the path for another 35mins to…

2.30 Maison Forestière de l'Estagnole, 1479m. Ignore the track left but continue E, avoiding another path to the left. Climb through the trees, steeply at times, to arrive at the open area at…

3.30 Col de la Cirère, 1731m. *The sign seems to indicate that it is a long way to the mines but that is not so.* Go SSE from the pass and ignore a path left, continuing ESE. The path comes down to a track. Turn right, S, and follow the track around to some old buildings where a road begins. Follow the road down to the…

4.00 Auberge du Batère, 1500m. *Marked as Mines de fer de Batère on maps. Just beyond the auberge entrance is the gîte, which should be open, even in the owners' absence. Excellent meals provided (Tel: 04.68.39.12.01).*

Day 47: Mines de Batère to Moulin de la Palette

Please refer to comments at the start of Day 46.

Distance:	20.6km (12.8 miles)
Height gain:	629m
Height loss:	1468m
Time:	5hrs 30mins
Maps:	IGN Carte de Randonnées No. 10

0.00 Auberge du Batère, 1500m. Go 800m down the road to where the road turns right with a track on the left. *The next part is reputed to be poorly marked but I did not find it so.* Take the path, E, that goes down to and follows a stream, post markers across grass. The trail turns towards the S and much later crosses a track before joining another that is followed S. This turns to the N and then back to the SE to lead to an old building…

1.10 Els Vigorats, 884m. Follow the path around to the left, which crosses a track within a few minutes. Continue SE, passing a stream and pool to a junction. Take the centre path, avoiding those on either side, that climbs S. At the top of the climb it meets a track. Go along the track, SE, soon taking a path to the left that climbs above the track to another track. Turn right, continuing past a track on the right and go along the track SE, soon passing beneath a high-tension wire. About 400m later take the narrower track on the right, SE, ignoring one coming from the right. Then take a path SE to join another old track that becomes a path once more and on down to a road. Turn left, SSW, and then left and left again, though a barrier to a square. *The GR is routed down an alleyway to the left, around the centre of town, before taking to the Passage de la Coquinère to reach the bus stop below the town.* For the bars and shop, go straight on to…

2.55 Arles-sur-Tech, 282m. *It appears that the cheaper*

Note

The route of the GR10, from Arles to just below Roc de France, was being surveyed during the autumn of 2001. The new FFRP guide showing the new route is due to be released in the summer of 2002. Please note that this Pyrénées Orientales section has been given a new reference, Ref. 1092 (not 1089 as it was previously). The statistics for Days 47 and 48 are therefore estimated. However, information gleaned from the surveyor, whom I met at Montalba, has allowed me to show the most likely routes on the sketch maps and to give some description of the most likely 'C' route.

Please also note that paths on the ground are not always shown, even on the 1:25,000 map. The various routes on the sketch maps have been indicated. A shows the old route; B the temporary diversion of 2001; C the expected new route; and D the track alternative that joins the C route below the abandoned Moli Serradou. For those electing to stay in Amélie, the best way to reach the GR10 again would be to climb the D53 road south to locate signposts, paths and tracks to la Chapelle Santa Engràcia.

The newly published FFRP guide Ref. 1092 still does not show the new route from Arles to Roc de France. However, the sketch map no. 48 route 'C' above Montalba has been chosen and marked via Mouli Serradou and Coll Cerda to Col du Puits-de-la-Neige, below Roc de France. The French guide advice is to follow the extra clearly marked trail. However, if you feel adventurous, you can save 200m of ascent and 2km of distance by crossing the River Tech, E of the town. Turn along a track past buildings to a narrow road. Turn right and climb the road, turning sharp left, NE. Just before the end of the road, with a farm up and to the left, there is a sign-posted path to Santa Engracia on the right. A short way up this path, look for a left turn, climbing to level area. Turn right, SE, climbing past →

accommodation, above the bar le Commerce, has closed. The Hôtel les Glycines in the SE part of town, near to the Spar shop, tends to be full and/or expensive. The jaded accommodation does not entirely live up to its sense of grandeur. On the road below this hotel is the bus stop. There is a bus to Amélie just after 12 midday and another at 4pm that best serve those arriving from the Auberge du Batère. There is a tourist office and several shops for food. Take care to locate the new route from Arles. From the bus stop the old route is probably followed E to cross the bridge over the River Tech. Then

→ a pylon to join a trail to the right. (This also climbs from the road but the start is not clear). Turn left, climbing eastwards to join with the trail coming from Col de Paracolls. Turn left and follow waymarks.

turn off left to join with a local road, turning right. Shortly, after a sharp left bend, take the path on the right that climbs all the way to the ridge above Amélie. The diversion route joins from the right and almost immediately turns right towards the chapel. Shortly you reach…

4.10 Chapelle de Santa Engràcia, 653m. *The surveyor indicated a high-level traverse, generally SSE, to Mas Pagris. A path is shown on the 1:25,000 map turning S just before the chapel but not continuing all the way. However, an old wooden signpost does point to Mas Pagris up a steep path to the right. At this point I followed the diversion.* Follow this high-level traverse which eventually descends to…

4.50 Mas Pagris, 500m. *No accommodation and meals reported in 2001, but this may change if the GR10 is routed past the hamlet.* Go down to the D53b road and turn right. Just after the bridge take the path on the right that avoids a large loop of the road. Upon reaching the road again, continue climbing the path on the other side and take a sharp right turn some metres later. This soon leads to the old GR10. Turn left to reach Montalba, but turn right and backtrack along the old GR10 to the D53b yet once more. Turn left, SSW, and follow for about 1km to…

Profile - Day 47

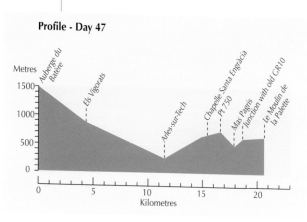

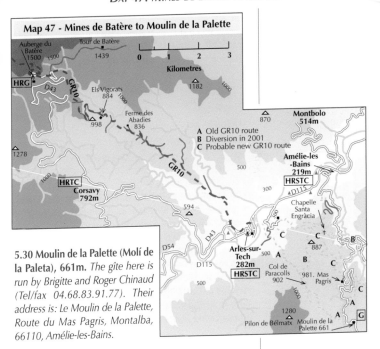

Map 47 - Mines de Batère to Moulin de la Palette

Auberge du Batère 1500
Tour de Batère 1439
HRG
D43
GR10
Els Vigorats 884
998
Ferme des Abadies 836
1278
HRTC
Corsavy 792m
GR10
1182
870
Montbolo 514m

A Old GR10 route
B Diversion in 2001
C Probable new GR10 route

Amélie-les-Bains 219m
HRSTC

Chapelle Santa Engràcia

594

Arles-sur-Tech 282m
HRSTC

D54

D115

Col de Paracolls 902

981. Mas Pagris

887

1280
Pilon de Bélmatx

Moulin de la Palette 661

G

5.30 Moulin de la Palette (Molí de la Paleta), 661m. *The gîte here is run by Brigitte and Roger Chinaud (Tel/fax 04.68.83.91.77). Their address is: Le Moulin de la Palette, Route du Mas Pagris, Montalba, 66110, Amélie-les-Bains.*

Day 48: Moulin de la Palette to Las Illas

Please refer to the comments at the start of Day 47.

Distance:	21km (13 miles)
Height gain:	902m
Height loss:	1013m
Time:	7hrs 05mins
Maps:	IGN Carte de Randonnées No. 10

0.00 Moulin de la Palette (Molí de la Paleta), 661m.
Retrace one's steps along the road and path to where the old GR10 was met yesterday. Turn right and follow the path SE and down to cross the Ravin de la Coume (Coma). Climb N a little then descend to…

0.45 Montalba d'Amélie, 543m. *Water point. The old route went E down the road, crossed the valley and climbed to Can Felix. Two new ways were being considered from Montalba to below Roc de France (Roc de Frausa). One way would go down the road to pick up*

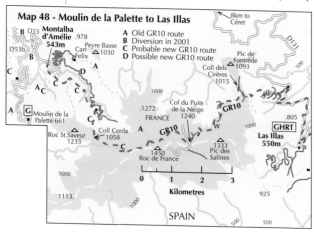

Map 48 - Moulin de la Palette to Las Illas

A Old GR10 route
B Diversion in 2001
C Probable new GR10 route
D Possible new GR10 route

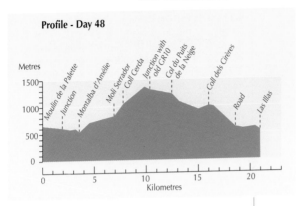

Profile - Day 48

the track on the other side of the River Montdony. This climbs to the old Moli Serrador. The other, described here, takes the path SE immediately above the water point. From the water point take the path climbing SE, and as it levels and continues straight on, take the path climbing on the right. About 20mins from Montalba, at another junction, avoid the path climbing steeply to the right and take the one going left, E, around the mountainside. Follow this to the track and turn right, SE. Sign to Coll Cerda. Fifteen minutes later, turn right, SSW, through a barrier and NW to...

1.55 Moli Serrador, 833m. With the abandoned mill on the right, climb up a dirt bank, through a hedge and follow the path, used by cattle, S, to...

2.40 Coll Cerda, 1058m. Identified by a signpost. Turn left, SE, and climb through the bushes to the open woodland on the E slopes of Roc de France. The path climbing steeply through the wood, SE and then E, was not always clear but was adequately marked by small cairns. Avoid any turns to the right and the ridge and also a turn left until a clear path turns left across the slope of a NW ridge from the Roc. This leads to...

4.00 Junction with old GR10, 1320m. Turn right, SE, and follow the contouring path, generally E, to the road at...

4.20 Col du Puits de la Neige, 1240m. *The route is quite complex to the D131 road that goes to Las Illas.* From the road, take the path NE below the rocks. This soon joins a junction of tracks and the path continues NE. About 30mins later a water point is passed and the path joins a track. Turn left, N, for a short distance and then take the path right, also N. Within a few minutes the path joins a track again. Turn right, ignoring a turn to the left, and the track becomes a path. A few minutes later continue NE, ignoring a path to the left. Ten minutes later take the **right** fork that climbs NE to soon join a track at…

5.25 Coll dels Cirères, 1015m. Turn sharp right, SE, and soon take the track left, E. This becomes a path that goes left at a junction, NE. Soon take another **left** branch, NNE and shortly a right one, ESE. This path then crosses four tracks, generally in a SE direction, before turning left on another, NE. This track turns to the ESE; ignore a track on the left. A few minutes later, turn left, E, at a junction. This track makes a loop to the N, crossing another track, before turning S and then SE to another junction. Turn left, N, and follow through bends past a farm to the road. Turn right, SW, and follow as it goes down to cross the river and then climbs on the other side before descending all the way to a junction. Turn right to take the road spur to…

7.05 Las Illas, 550m. *The gîte is beside the mairie and telephone box. Mme Martinez, who looks after the gîte, lives a few houses to the N. Continuing to the road end one arrives at the hotel/restaurant and bar. A pleasant and easy diversion can be made to La Vajol, on a rest day, on the GR11 in Spain by following the track S to the border. Turn left and follow the track down to the road and on to La Vajol, which also has a restaurant but no accommodation.*

Day 49: Las Illas to Chalet de l'Albère (Col de l'Oullat)

Distance:	24.8km (15.4 miles)
Height gain:	959m
Height loss:	573m
Time:	5hrs 50mins
Maps:	IGN Carte de Randonnées Nos. 10 & 11

A long day, but easy ground makes for a fast passage. The tourist trap of Le Perthus enables replenishment of supplies and a meal if required, but it is a place to pass through rather than stay. There is little traffic on the road to St-Martin, so the climb, though long, is pleasant.

0.00 Las Illas, 550m. Go NNE down the road from the gîte and take the road on the right, and then turn right again at the next junction. Climb the long zigzags, being careful to avoid all the access roads both left and right by looking for the confirming marks. The road arrives at the...

0.45 Col du Figuier, 685m. *The road has now been extended.* From the signpost, ignore the two tracks on the right and go NE. Ignore turnings left and right and then the road becomes a track, N. Ignore a track left and follow the main track, generally NE. The sketch map shows the turnings to avoid but one, 500m after Mas Nou, is important. Turn right here, ESE, as the main track

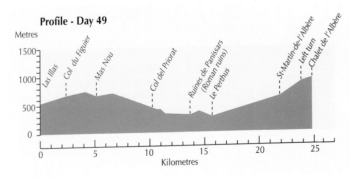

Profile - Day 49

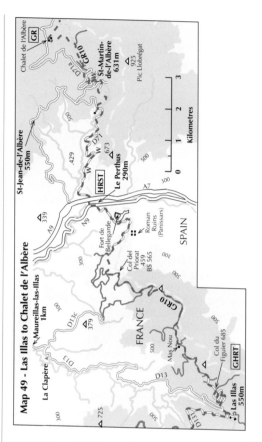

Map 49 - Las Illas to Chalet de l'Albère

appears to go N. The track now follows the border, leaving it before returning at...

2.10 Col del Priorat, 459m. *Border stone 565 identifies the spot.* Go NNW for 500m and at a junction, take the path on the right, climbing E. Several minutes later it meets a track. Turn right, SE and follow to the road. The road is followed past a farm and then some Roman ruins to climb N around the fort and down into...

3.20 Le Perthus, 290m. *This is the last reprovisioning* *point before Banyuls. It is necessary to go downhill at the main road to find the supermarket.* From the point of entry, go N about 200m where a right turn is marked that leads under the motorway and onto the start of the long climb to St-Martin. *There are various water points along the way.* About an hour or so from Le Perthus and just past the track to Mas Reste, take the path right, E. *The next section to and through St-Martin is quite complex.* In 2mins take a sharp turn left, N, leaving the main path. The path curves round to the E, and in a few minutes joins a road. Go ESE along the road to a junction. Go straight across the junction into a field and climb the edge of the field to the road above. Turn left, N, past the church at...

4.50 St-Martin-de-l'Albère, 631m. Pass a font on the right to join the main road, the D71a. Follow this W then N and take a track on the right going NNE. Soon, at a junction on a bend, take the right-hand fork in the track and immediately a path on the left through the bushes, N. In a few minutes this goes across the road, ENE, and then a second time NE. Cross one track, and then another above. The path climbs to a junction where the track on the right curves round to the frontier. One path, less used now, passes through bushes straight ahead, while the other turns left, signed to Col de l'Oullat. Take this path through the wood to...

5.50 Chalet de l'Albère (Col de l'Oullat), 936m. *Gîte and restaurant with views back to the Canigou.*

Day 50: Chalet de l'Albère (Col de l'Oullat) to Banyuls-sur-Mer

The final day! The frontier ridge is followed for half the day, with the long walk out to the coast beyond. But there's a sting in the tail here: in the unlikely event of cloud this route would be very difficult to find.

Distance:	24.2km (15 miles)
Height gain:	646m
Height loss:	1582m
Time:	6hrs 35mins
Maps:	IGN Carte de Randonnées No. 11

0.00 Chalet de l'Albère (Col de l'Oullat), 936m. Go the few metres to the road and take the ascending path on the right, ESE, through the tall trees of the Forêt d'Albère. This leads to just below the frontier. Ignore the waymarks above, as these only lead down again, but turn left and walk along the level to the road and pass of Col des Trois Termes (1110m). Do not go up the road as indicated in the French guide but take to the path between the frontier and the road. Climb NE all the way to the TV relay station on the top of…

0.50 Pic Néoulous, 1256m. Pass to the left of the station and follow the track and then path around to the right

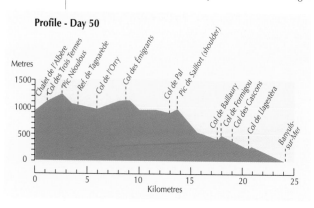

Profile - Day 50

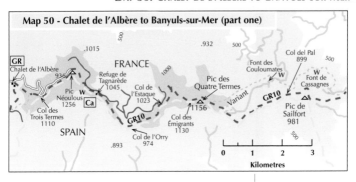

Map 50 - Chalet de l'Albère to Banyuls-sur-Mer (part one)

and SSE. Go steeply down to a water point. *The water will need sterilising.* Continue along the path, above the track on the left, to the...

1.15 Refuge de Tagnarède, 1045m. *CAF hut without guardian.* Just after the hut, take the left fork and then a right one, SE, and right again to the crest to follow frontier fence. Twenty-five minutes later leave the main path at the pass, Col de l'Orry (974m), and climb ENE; no real path, but post markers on the level bits. Another 15 minutes on follow the path N to marks, eventually to reach a corner of the fence at the Col de l'Estaque (1023m). *A variant climbs the frontier ridge to the top of Pic des Pradets (1175m).* The GR climbs NE with no path at first but post markers. Ten minutes later ignore a path to the left in the wood and then follow the path round to the SE, ignoring another path left. At a junction, take the path on the right, SSE, and in a few minutes arrive at the top of the climb and on to a signpost at...

2.35 Col des Émigrants, 1130m. Continue E and pass to the left of the Pic des Quatre Termes (1156m). *A variant goes off left just after the summit, and the broken ground and many trails can be confusing, so take care. The GR goes down to the wood on the right, crosses a stream and on to the frontier before turning to the NE. The variant, marked on the sketch map, is probably used in search of water at the Font de Couloumates in exteme*

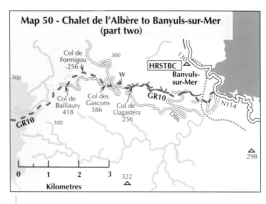

Map 50 - Chalet de l'Albère to Banyuls-sur-Mer (part two)

heat. As the path starts to go SE downhill, take a right fork and continue down SE. At a junction below, turn right, cross the stream and go on SSE. Ten minutes later, at a level bit turn left, NE, and after 15mins, at a fork, take the lower of the two paths. Fifteen minutes later, at the Col del Pal (899m), turn right off the path, to climb steeply E and ENE to a pass between rocks on the saddle of...

3.50 Pic de Sailfort, 981m. Go SE to a post and then S to locate the very steep descent. *A stone wind shelter soon appears on the left, useful if indeed it is windy and a lunch stop due.* The trail goes down to the ridge that is followed, first on one side then the other. Keep a close eye out for a sharp turn down to the left, N, as this could be easily missed. This then joins the variant route coming from the left. Turn right and follow the path NE, over an old watercourse, for 2km. This comes to a road that is followed right, E, for about 150m, passing a clear path going off and down to the left, to reach a gate at the Col de Baillaury (418m). *A variant continues along the winding road beyond the gate.* The GR climbs a path on the left, NE, over the rocky ridge, passing through the Col de Formigou (256m) and then along an arid, fairly level path before going down steeply to the road at...

5.15 Col des Gascons, 386m. Go 50m E down the road

before taking the steep path down left that continues E. *Not along the road as in the French guide.* It crosses the road twice before passing a water point on a level section and comes to the road again. Follow the road E to...

5.40 Col de Llagastèra, 256m. *Attention is again needed as the route takes to a number of tracks through the vineyards.* Take the track NE, then a right fork E, continuing E and ignoring two other tracks to the left. Five minutes later take a right fork and then a path right, SE to the track below. Turn right, W, following the track through three bends and to the E, passing two further tracks on the left, where the track turns SE. In about 100m take a path on the right, ESE, that soon joins a track and just as quickly turns off SE. This soon comes to a road. Cross it and go down the one opposite and take the track on the right, E. In a few minutes take the path off right, SE to a road. Turn left and underneath the railway line and at the junction, turn left and follow to the beach! *The railway station is above the town to the WNW.*

Banyuls-sur-Mer

GR10 VARIANTS

Unfortunately I have not been able to walk the many GR10 variants. However, these are listed below as they occur on a daily basis, with a brief description of the routes. The three-day option from Cauterets to Luz-St-Sauveur is given more coverage as I know the first and upper parts quite well.

DAY 8 COL BAGARGIAK TO LARRAU

Those needing either a shop or campsite may like to try the variant directly to Larrau, using the road and trails across some of the bends. It is also recommended when low cloud prevails. Not waymarked! Allow 2hrs 30mins.

From the office at the Col de Bagargiak, take the signposted road down SE towards Larrau. Just after the first sharp right-hand bend, take the path on the left that meets the road a few minutes later. Go straight across down a track that joins the road at a sharp bend. Follow the road down E and after 1km turn off left, up to the left of Pt 921, and then make your own way down to Forges de Larrau (506m). Continue along the road for about 800m and then take the track on the left to the Granges de Soule. Cross a field and continue to Larrau.

DAY 9 LOGIBAR TO ST-ENGRÂCE VIA HOLZATÉ RAVINE

This route takes more than an hour longer than the normal way. It is essential to acertain whether the suspension bridge is open or not. The route is closed during the hunting season. Not waymarked! Allow 2hrs 30mins to join the GR10.

Instead of climbing above the bridge behind the auberge, turn right and follow the well-worn trail on the right side of the valley. This climbs to the N wall of the ravine and the suspension bridge in about 45mins. Cross the bridge with care and continue on the other side to the SE, first climbing up the slope ahead. The clear path eventually leads to a bridge where a crossing is made back to the N side again. Follow the path and track N to the Plateau Ardakhotchia.

Day 9 Logibar to St-Engrâce via E side of Kakouéta ravine

From the farm Anhaou turn right and follow the track past the edge of a wood before descending towards the head of the ravine down steep grass. Climb E through the wood to the farm Larrégorry (1227m). The track goes generally N, well above the E of the ravine. Much later the trail turns SE, crosses an old bridge and continues NNE, then E to the bridge le Pont de Gaztélugar (540m). Take the road up left to another bridge, and turn left to the gîte at St-Engrâce.

This variant avoids the long road ascent to the gîte at St-Engrâce, but waymaking had not been renewed for some time. I am led to believe that this has now been remedied. It also takes over an hour longer than the present route. Allow about 4hrs or more.

Day 10 St-Engrâce to Arette-la Pierre-St-Martin via Col de Suscouse

Take the road WSW from the gîte and then the sharp turn right along the road D113 to the ENE. This can be followed all the way to Col de Suscouse, though 3km of a loop can be avoided by a trail going E at about 950m. From the col, follow the yellow-and-red marks of the Tour de Barétous to the S. These lead to the D132 that is followed, SE, up to the ski station.

In the event of low cloud causing concern with navigation, this way can be an easier option. Allow about 4hrs for the route.

Day 17 Cauterets to Luz-St-Sauveur via the Hourquette d'Ossoue

Hourquette d'Ossoue after first winter snow

This is a three-day excursion from Cauterets to view the spectacular scenery of Vignemale and to climb the high pass of Hourquette d'Ossoue (2734m) before the no-less-scenic route down to below Gavarnie and then north back to Luz. It was once viewed as a variant but now seems to be given equal status with the direct route. However, expect severe snow conditions if this is walked as part of a coast-to-coast traverse from the W and starting in early to mid June. The road south from Cauterets can be followed, or a similar path on the W side of the valley. It takes about 6hrs 45mins to the Refuge de Bayssellance and 6hrs 20mins to the gîte de Saugué, though the Chalet-Refuge de Grange de Holle is reached earlier. Then allow about 5hrs 50mins from the gîte to Luz.

From where the GR10 passes the steps above the thermal baths, continue across the GR main route to reach a path going S across the wooded hillside. This drops down to the Latour valley, crosses it and climbs steeply up to the cafés and shops at La Raillère (1044m). Just above the buildings the other trail joins from the right along a track, and the trail climbs SW up the true left side of the Jéret valley and beside the many cascades. At the Pont d'Espagne a track climbs to the top of the télésiège at the Lac de Gaube, but the GR takes the path that starts 100m down the road on the right just after a bridge and cascade. Climb the path S, steep at first, all the way to Lac de Gaube (1725m). Pass around the W side of the lake, passing Cabane de Pinet (1783m), continuing S to a small bridge that conducts pedestrians to the left bank of the stream. The sheer N face of Vignemale, the Pique Longue, comes into view and the clear trail continues towards it, passing a camping area, until it reaches Refuge des Oulettes de Gaube (2151m). *Overnight camping allowed between 1900 and 0900hrs.* Cross beneath the refuge to the right side of the valley and follow this round to the zigzags climbing E up the steep mountainside. Much higher, a junction is reached where the right path is taken. *The other continues ENE to the Col d'Arraillé, Refuge d'Estom and Cauterets.* An ascending traverse is followed S until more zigzags climb SE over very rough and steep ground to the Hourquette d'Ossoue (2734m). *In clear weather the Refuge Bayssellance can be seen below to the E. A short, easy climb can be made to the summit of Petit Vignemale (3032m). However, at this altitude the steep slope seems very hard to surmount to an unexpected airy summit in close proximity to sheer crags sweeping down to the glacier below.* Go E down to the Refuge Bayssellance (2651m). *This is the highest guarded refuge in the Pyrenees. Booking in advance recommended for weekends and during the summer holidays.* Below the hut, in a stream valley, the clear path goes ESE then SW down to Grottes de Bellevue, some small caves hewn in the rock. *These are part of the system of caves that Count*

Russell engineered to provide accommodation for overnight stops and for entertaining friends on Vignemale's high slopes. These are still used for a rather cold overnight bivvy. From the caves, continue E, then S down the W side of the Barranco d'Ossoue, and then E again to cross a small bridge to the left side of the wide open area of the Oulettes d'Ossoue (1866m). Go past the left-hand side of the lake to a small hut where an overnight stop can usually be made. *A bivouac is not permitted around the lake but you can put up a small tent beside the cabane. The track going E from here becomes a road that goes all the way to Gavarnie and cuts the GR trail about 2km before the village. This is very much easier than following the GR trail.* The GR10 crosses a bridge below the dam and goes SSE, climbing to a shepherd's hut before crossing the Canou stream by another bridge. Then, contouring the mountainside NE, SE and S, the trail leads to the Cabane de Sausse-Desus (1900m). Cross the stream by a footbridge and continue the contouring to the E, leaving the Parque National. The trail begins to descend, passing the ruined Cabane des

Lac de Gaube

My son on Petit Vignemale

Tousaous and then crosses above very steep slopes to the left to pass across a road twice, with the Refuge Grange de Holle (1480m) on the right. *Open all year with the exception of November. To reach Gavarnie go E down the road.* From the refuge go N up to the Couret de Holle (1510m), and then down N to the Gave d'Ossoue at Pont de Saint-Savin (1436m). *Camping possible.* Cross the bridge and climb E to cross the road coming from the Ossoue dam. *The road can be followed down to Gavarnie.* The trail turns to the N beside pylons – not the place to be during an electric storm. Continue N, avoiding several tracks to the right to meet a road that leads to the gîte d'étape de Saugré, (1610m). From the gîte go N for 200m before taking a path on the left beside a wall that goes W to cross the Gave d'Aspé before climbing NNE and then NE to a col on the shoulder of Soum Haut, the Col de Suberpeyre (1725m). The trail then makes a long sweep to the W and then back to the ENE, passing the Granges de Bué (1482m) before crossing the Gave de Cestrède below the road at the Pont de Balit (1215m). Continue NE, crossing another bridge and on to Trimbareilles (1000m). Take the road N to the

D921 at the N end of Pragnères. Follow the D921 N to the first junction. Turn left to the campsite and café Saint-Bazerque. Just before the café, turn right and follow the trail, just above the road, NNW to the hamlet of Sia and then on to the wooden Croix de Sia at a high point of the trail. Continue N, carefully following the marks as there are many other pathways, on to the road and GR10 main route above St-Sauveur. Follow the description at the end of Day 17.

Day 20 GR10C, Junction above Cabane de Bastan to Artigues-de-Gripp

The trail goes N from above the Bastan cabane, turning NE to pass the Lac Bastan Inferior (2141m). The trail turns N again to pass the small Le Laquet (2197m) and on past the Lac de Milieu to the Refuge de Bastan (2240m). Continue N past the W side of the last Bastan lake, Lac Supérieur (2260m), to the rugged Hourquette de Bastanet (2507m). The trail quickly loses height passing between the Lacs de Hourquette (2405m) where the trail passes the NE side of the larger one. *Camping again now possible.* At the end of the large lake, avoid the clear trail left but continue N to Lac Campana. On the E side is the Refuge de Campana (2225m). Go N and pass along the NE side of Lac de Grésiolles and then the W side of reservoir below. Continue to a junction and turn right, following the path NE and then NNW to Atrigues-de-Gripp (1200m).

This is an access route from the Ardour valley, but snow persists for 10 months on the Hourquette de Bastanet (2507m). Camping spots can be found as far as the upper Bastan lake. Allow about 4hrs to 4hrs 30 mins.

Day 27 GR10E, Junction on the climb to Col de l'Arech to Gîte de Bonac

From the variant sign take the path, generally N, that contours the mountainside. Avoiding the path that descends to the W, turn E to a ridge and on down to the Col de Cassaings (1497m). Go N beyond the cabane, to the W of the ridge, again contouring the slope. After about 2km the path enters a wood and joins a track. Much later, look out for a turn left that goes down NW and turns right to the ridge again. Take the track on the right to the Cabane de l'Arraing (1129m), 10m above

This route then joins the GR10 at Étang de Bethmale on Day 29. This would be an option if a tent is not carried. Allow 2hrs 50mins to Bonac and 3hrs 40mins to Étang de Bethmale.

the track. Much later, as the track turns to the S, take off left, NW and down to Bonac (706m). Go E from the church along the D4 and take the trail left up to the D704. Turn left into Samiac and follow the D704 to Uchentein (950m). From here a trail goes ENE to a stream and then SE down towards the D4, but turns NE before crossing a road and on down to the D4, which is followed N for 500m. Take the dirt track on the right SSE to Bouche (700m) and another gîte. Across the valley the D17 goes all the way to Étang de Bethmale, but the GR10E follows a series of paths and tracks on the SW side. Scant directions are available so follow the marks carefully, E at first and then generally SE to Étang de Bethmale (1060m).

DAY 29 GR10D, COL D'AUÉDOLE TO ESTOURS

Take the level path on the right. the lower of the two seen as the upper one goes to the Étang d'Eychelle. The path passes the outlet gully from the étang mentioned above and passes a shoulder with steep crags above and below. Go down to the E at the foot of the crags. The path gently climbs to the NE to reach the Crête de Balam and down to the Pas de la Core. Take the trail, SE, with the road on the left and ridge to the right. Go into the wood, and about 1km later the trail turns SW to the Cabane de Luzurs. *A place to sleep but with no water.* Climb above the hut, come out onto the open mountainside to contour at about 1600m to Cabane de Casabède. Continue ESE to the Col du Soularil (1579m). Go down SE to find a path at 1500m that goes S and SW to Cabane de Subera with a water supply. *One part is available to walkers.* Leave the path and go down, NE, along the right side of the stream, the Ruisseau de Lameza, past the farm of the same name and follow the stream to the SE. *This is now the Ruisseau d'Arros.* Cross the river by the footbridge and continue to the Carrièrre de Marbre d'Estours at the junction of the Arros and Estours streams. Cross the bridge to the GR10.

The first part is a short cut to the Pas de la Core, only to be used in settled and fine weather. It was once the course of the GR10. From the Pas de la Core it goes south in wide loops to the Cabane de Subera, turning east-north-east and then south-east to the junction of the Rivers Estours and Arros, where it joins with the GR10. Allow 1hr 15mins to the Pas de la Core and about 4hrs 15mins to Estours.

DAY 34 GR10A, ÉTANG D'IZOURT TO REFUGE DE FOURCAT

Go S around the E side of Étang d'Izourt and climb S to the Orri de la Caudière (1942m). Cross the stream and climb the path, generally SSW, to the large cairns guarding the entrance to the cirque, the Hommes de Pierres (2350m). Continue SSW past the W side of Petit Étang de Fourcat (2339m). Climb S to overlook Étang de Fourcat (2420m), then turn left, E and climb to the Refuge du Forcat (2445m). Retrace one's steps to the Orri de la Caudière, and then either return to the Étang d'Izourt or take the path right that climbs above the Étang d'Izourt. *This crosses steep ground with vertical drops and is only recommended in fine weather.* Just follow the path to the junction with the GR10.

This is an extension of Day 34 to reach the refuge as required. Allow about 2hrs 45mins to the refuge and 1hr 50mins to the GR10.

DAY 34 GR10B, FROM THE STÈLE TO COL D'ESQUÉRUS

Follow the level path past the Source de Brosquet (1413m) and continue to the parking area at the closed Refuge de la Prade. Take the road NE for 500m and then the track on the right that continues above the road. After about 1km the track bears right to Col d'Esquérus (1467m).

This track contours the valley above Goulier, thus avoiding the only accommodation! Allow about 2hrs 30mins.

FACILITIES LIST

DAY	LOCATION	GÎTE	HOTEL OR ROOMS	REST.	SHOP	BANK	REFUGE	CAMPSITE	CABIN
1	Hendaye		x	x	x	x		x	
	Biriatou		x	x					
	Venta d'Inzola			x	x				
	Olhette	x	x	x					
2	Sare	x	x	x	x			x	
	Venta Beruet (Dancharia)			x	x				
	Aïnhoa		x	x				x	
3	Ferme Esteben	x		x	x			x	
	Bidarray	x	x	x	x			x	
4	St-Étienne	x	x	x	x			x	
5	Lasse		x	x					
	St-Jean-Pied-de-Port	x	x	x	x	x		x	
6	Estérençuby	x	x	x					
7	Chalet Pedro		x	x	x				
	Col Bagargiak (Chalets d'Irati)	x		x				x	x
8	Logibar (Larrau)	x	x	x	x				
9	Ste-Engrâce	x	x	x				x	
10	Arette-la Pierre-St-Martin		(x)	(x)	(x)		x	x	
11	Cne du Cap de la Baitch								x
	Refuge de Labérouat						(x)		
12	Lescun	x	x	x	x			x	
	Plateau de Lhers	x						x	
	Borce	x			x			x	
	Etsaut	x	x	x	x				
13	Cne de la Baigt de St-Cours								x

DAY	LOCATION	GÎTE	HOTEL OR ROOMS	REST.	SHOP	BANK	REFUGE	CAMPSITE	CABIN
	Refuge d'Ayous						x		
	Lac de Bious-Artigues						x	x	
	Gabas		x	x	x		x		
14	Cabanes de Cézy								x
	Gourette		(x)	(x)	(x)	(x)	x	(x)	
15	Arrens-Marsous	x	x	x	x			x	
16	Estaing							x	
	Les Viellettes	x		x					
	Lac d'Estaing		x	x					
	Lac d'Illhéou						x		
	Cauterets	x	x	x	x	x		x	
17	Grust	x	x	x					
	Sazos							x	
	St-Sauveur		x	x					
	Luz-St-Sauveur	x	x	x	x	x		x	
18	Bolou	x							
	Barèges	x	x	x	x			x	
19	Cne d'Aygues-Cluses								x
	Lac d'Aubert							x	
	(Chalet-Hôtel d'Oredon)		x	x			x		
	Chalet-Hôtel de l'Oule		x	x			x		
20	Vielle-Aure		x	x	x			x	
	(St-Lary-Soulan)		x	x	x	x		x	
	(Sailhan)	x							
21	Azet	x	x	x					
	Loudenvielle		x	x	x			x	
	Germ	x						x	

DAY	LOCATION	GÎTE	HOTEL OR ROOMS	REST.	SHOP	BANK	REFUGE	CAMPSITE	CABIN
22	Cne d'Ourtiga								x
	Granges d'Astau	x							
	Lac d'Oô						x		
23	(Réfuge d'Espingo)						x		
	Superbagnères		x	x					x
	Bagnères de Luchon	x	x	x	x	x		x	
24	Artigue			x					x
	Cne de Peyrahitta								x
	Cnes des Courraus								x
	Cne d'Artigue								x
	Cne d'Artiguessans								x
25	Fos	x		x				x	
	Melles		x	x					x
	Cne d'Uls								x
	Ref de l'Étang d'Araing						x		x
26	Cne de Bentaillou								x
	Eylie-d'en-Haut	x							
27	Cne de l'Arech								x
	Cne de Grauillès								x
	Cne de Besset								x
28	Cne du Trapech du Milieu								x
	Cne de l'Artigue								x
	Ref du Pla de la Lau								x
	Cne d' Aouen								x
29	Cne de Clot d'Eliet								x
	Cne de Tariolle								x
	Esbints	x							

	1	2	3	4	5	6	7	8
(Seix)					(x)			
Aunac							x	
30 (Pont de la Taule)	x					x	x	
Ref d'Aula								
Rouze								x
31 St-Lizier-d'Ustou	x		x		x	x	x	
(Bidous)								x
32 Aulus-les-Bains	x		x		x	x	x	x
Ref des Bassiès				x		x		
33 (Auzat)					x	x	x	
(Vicdessos)			x		x	x	x	
Marc						x	x	
Mounicou								x
34 Ref de Prunadière	x							
Barage de l'Étang d'Izourt	x							
(Ref de l'Étang Fourcat)	x			x				
Goulier								x
35 Cne Col de Grail	x							
Siguer								x
36 Ref de Clarans	x							
37 Cne d'Artaran	x							
Plateau de Beille	x					x		
(Cne du Rieutort)	x							
(Cne d'Embizon)	x							
Refuge de Rulhe					x			
38 Mérens-les-Vals	x				x	x	x	
39 Ref des Bésines	x			x				x
(Cabane du Sola)	x							x

DAY	LOCATION	GÎTE	HOTEL OR ROOMS	REST.	SHOP	BANK	REFUGE	CAMPSITE	CABIN
40	Lac des Bouillouses		x	x			x		
41	Abri de l'Étang de la Pradeille								x
	Superbolquère	x							
	Bolquère		x	x	x				
	Col de la Perche	x	x	x					
	La Cabanasse				x			x	
	Planès	x							
42	Ref de l'Orry								x
	Ref Ras de la Carança						x		
43	Mantet	x							
44	Py	x			x				
	Ref de Marailles						x		
45	Ref de Bonne-Aigue								x
	Chalet-Hôtel de Cortalets		x	x			x		
46	Abri du Pinatell								x
	Maison Forestière de l'Estagnole								x
	Mines de Batères	x		x					
47	Arles-sur-Tech	x	x	x	x				
	Moulin de la Palette							x	
48	Las Illas	x	x	x					
49	Le Perthus		x	x	x	x			
	Col de l'Ouillat-Chalet de l'Albère	x		x					
50	Ref de la Tagnarède								x
	Banyuls-sur-Mer		x	x	x	x		x	

VARIANTS – 3 DAYS VIA REF. BAYSSELLANCE

		C1	C2	C3	C4	C5	C6	C7	C8
17	La Raillère					X	X		
	Pont d'Espagne					X	X		
	Lac de Gaube					X	X	X	
	Cabane de Pinet	X							
	Oulettes de Gaube			X					
	Refuge Bayssellance			X					
	Chalet-refuge Grange de Holle			X					
	Gavarnie		X		X	X	X		
	Saugué					X	X		
	GR10C								
20	Refuge de Bastan			X			X		
	Refuge de Campana			X					
	Artigues-de-Gripp		X			X			
	GR10E								
27	Cabane de l'Arraing	X							
	Bonac							X	
	Bouche							X	
	GR10D								
29	Cabane de Luzurs	X							
	Cabane de Subera	X							
	GR10A								
34	Refuge du Fourcat			X					
	GR101								
15	Col de Soulor					X		X	
	Lourdes				X	X	X	X	

209

BIBLIOGRAPHY

Dubin, Marc.
The Pyrenees, The Rough Guide (Rough Guides, 3rd edition 1998)

Les Sentiers de Grande Randonnée Ref. 1086 – Pyrénées Occidentales
(Fédération Française de la Randonnée Pédestre, 1998)

Les Sentiers de Grande Randonnée Ref. 1091 – Pyrénées Centrales (Fédération
Française de la Randonnée Pédestre, 1998)

Les Sentiers de Grande Randonnée Ref. 1090 – Pyrénées Ariégeoises
(Fédération Française de la Randonnée Pédestre, 1998)

Les Sentiers de Grande Randonnée Ref. 1091 – Pyrénées Orientales (Fédération
Française de la Randonnée Pédestre, 1998)

Reynolds, Kev.
Walks and Climbs in The Pyrenees (Cicerone Press, 1993)

Streatfeild-James, Douglas.
Trekking in the Pyrenees (Trailblazer Publications, 2001)

Walking the Pyrenees, GR10 (Robertson McCarta; out of print but kindly loaned
by Michael Winterton)

NOTES

NOTES

NOTES

NOTES

NOTES

NOTES

LISTING OF CICERONE GUIDES

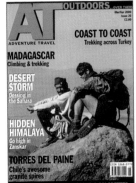

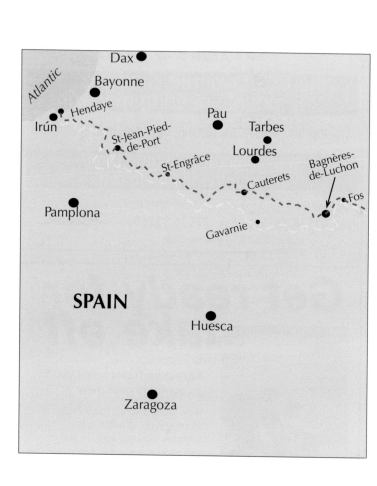

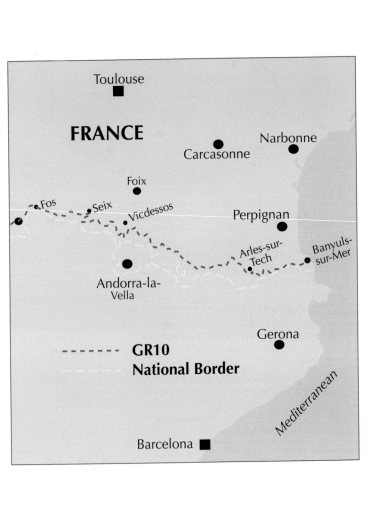

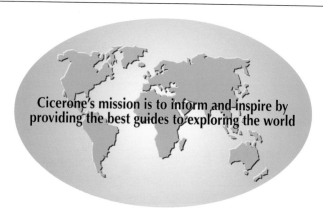

Cicerone's mission is to inform and inspire by
providing the best guides to exploring the world

Since its foundation over 30 years ago, Cicerone has specialised in
publishing guidebooks and has built a reputation for quality and reliability.
It now publishes nearly 300 guides to the major destinations for outdoor
enthusiasts, including Europe, UK and the rest of the world.

Written by leading and committed specialists, Cicerone guides are
recognised as the most authoritative. They are full of information, maps and
illustrations so that the user can plan and complete a successful and safe
trip or expedition – be it a long face climb, a walk over Lakeland fells, an
alpine traverse, a Himalayan trek or a ramble in the countryside.

With a thorough introduction to assist planning, clear diagrams, maps and
colour photographs to illustrate the terrain and route, and accurate and
detailed text, Cicerone guides are designed for ease of use and access to
the information.

If the facts on the ground change, or there is any aspect of a guide that you
think we can improve, we are always delighted to hear from you.

Cicerone Press
2 Police Square Milnthorpe Cumbria LA7 7PY
Tel:01539 562 069   Fax:01539 563 417
e-mail:info@cicerone.co.uk   web:www.cicerone.co.uk

CICERONE